Introvert Survival Tactics:

How to Make Friends, Be More Social, and Be Comfortable in Any Situation

(When You're All "People'd Out" and Just Want to Go Home and Watch TV Alone)

By Patrick King, Social Interaction Specialist at
www.PatrickKingConsulting.com

3

Table of Contents

6

Introduction

I don't want to be alone, I want to be left alone – Audrey Hepburn

I struggled for years with trying to perform a poor impersonation of an extrovert.

You've probably been there at some point. Remember the last time you were out late at night, and everyone else seem enthused to keep the party going, leading them to call you a party pooper because you want to sleep at three in the morning?

When you invite people over only to hope they leave after an hour or two, and preferring only small groups as opposed to large parties—also regretting hosting an event in the first place. Or when you actively turn down invitations for social events for no reason other than not feeling "up to it."

These tendencies were massively confusing for me because I had considered myself a socially capable person up to that point in my life. Sure, I was more shy and overweight as a teenager, but I had worked through most of those issues and could generally talk to anyone.

I had fallen into the trap of many: I mentally classified myself as an extrovert because I was socially capable. I hadn't stopped to think twice about whether that was how I *wanted* to be. Most societies (in the West, anyway) have a certain extrovert ideal, so I thought everything was working out great for me.

It's like someone who is seven feet tall and

good at basketball realizing that they don't really want to play professional basketball and who instead prefers to study accounting.

Naturally, that makes you question if wanting to spend time by yourself and *not* be that extrovert ideal makes you an unsuccessful deviant.

But it wasn't just me as an outlier. It turned out that a few of my friends were also like this and felt exactly how I felt about endless social obligations. Upon asking them, it turned out that a few more of *their friends* were just like me.

What we were missing about being labeled an introvert or extrovert was an understanding of the fundamental concept of the social battery and how it *normalized* us.

The social battery is the amount of social energy that we have at any given time. Not all batteries are created equally, as some are bigger and longer-lasting than others. Everyone has one, and everyone's runs out at some point. The big difference is what happens when the social battery runs out and requires recharging for both extroverts and introverts. An extrovert recharges by being around other people. They feed off the energy of others and use it to remind themselves that they can reach that level, too. Their social batteries are charged by other people. Being alone can actually drain their batteries and make them listless and unmotivated.

An introvert, by contrast, recharges by being alone. Being around others saps their social battery, and they need quiet, alone time to fill it back to where they feel they can interact with others again.

Ah, so that's why I needed to shut down and veg in front of the TV after long days and events.

That's really what the *introvert* label is about. It has nothing to do with how socially capable you are or even how much you enjoy social situations. It just has to do with how well you tolerate it. You can banter, verbally spar, and hobnob with the best of them; you just want to stop doing it sooner than others.

If you just feel that something is wrong with you because you don't always welcome the enormous parties, it's likely that you'll keep attempting to fit in with the extrovert ideal—and fail as miserably as a square peg trying to fit into a round hole. When this failure cycle repeats a few times, it's inevitable that your self-esteem and self-worth take hits.

The best part of my education on the introvert was to be at terms with who I was and not feel like I had to live up to a standard that was literally impossible for me. I didn't feel like I had to be someone I wasn't, and I could indulge in my introverted tendencies without guilt or a sense of failure. If you are left-handed and all the tools in the world are right-handed, it is natural to feel like there is something wrong with you.

Better yet, I learned there were actual strategies to both be myself and indulge in my social desires, so I could do more with less. It's a bit more complex than simply going home when you recognize that you're tired, but not much more so. I could shine brighter and for longer while not disturbing my introvert tendencies.

Hence the title: introvert survival tactics.

When I tell people I identify as an introvert now, people are always shocked by it. Really, it's just a combination of understanding how I tick and designing my life around it that lets me live to my potential. People say that 90 percent of the battle is simply being there, and mastering your temperament puts you in a position for success 90 percent more of the time.

Chapter 1. Understanding Introversion

As you've already read in the introduction of this book, there are a lot of misconceptions about what it means to be an introvert. I want to take this first chapter to clear them all up and shed some light onto who you are versus who you've been told you should be.

Misconceptions

While introverts make up a large portion of the population, and one that seems to increase every day, there are still a lot of misconceptions about this personality type. People assume that introverts are shy, are socially awkward, dislike people, and generally don't play well with others. They might also be seen as rude or unapproachable.

This stereotype may be understandable, since it cannot be denied that many introverted individuals do possess these traits. However, it is not true that all introverts are nervous, antisocial wrecks. Not all of them are timid and quiet. Being shy and anxious can accompany introversion, but it does not define it.

At their social peak, an introvert is indistinguishable from an extrovert—it's what they do afterward when they are tired that differentiates them. If you see someone who appears to be shy or unapproachable, chances are they are simply socially tapped out.

A person's activity alone is not an accurate indicator of whether he or she is an introvert. For instance, a party animal is not necessarily an extrovert. Being a loner most of the time does not make you an introvert. The same logic follows when I say that the person you see partying a lot may simply be an introvert living life outside his comfort zone. The person you always see alone may not necessarily be an introvert; she might be forced into that situation. That person may like spending their energy going outside; however, some circumstances beyond her control did not allow her to perform according to her desires.

People are adaptable and will rise to the occasion when necessary, but in the end, this leads to many an unrealized introvert trying to put on a poor impression of an extrovert for years and years. You might think you're weird or that something is wrong with you if you hate going to bars while all your friends love it—you just have a different personality than them.

In the same vein, many others use the term as a negative description, as if there was something fundamentally wrong with someone because they didn't want to hang out all night, every night. If you don't always crave additional socialization, you must border on antisocial and loner tendencies. As with everything, it is impossible to create a black and white delineation here. These notions of an introvert are completely wrong for a few reasons.

Introverts simply have a limited amount of social energy that they can devote to people and events. As aforementioned, this is measured by the concept of the *social battery*. Imagine a battery meter over an introvert's head draining slightly with every conversation they have and every question they answer. When it finally runs down to zero, they feel exhausted and need to recharge through isolation and avoidance of further social interaction. It can take anywhere from hours to days to weeks for an introvert's social battery to recharge.

Someone who is *shy or anxious or even depressed* doesn't dictate their actions based on their social battery. They do so because they are uncomfortable with themselves and thus other people. They lack confidence and feel that they are constantly judged and picked apart. They may even associate people with painful or unhappy experiences. Being social is a trigger point that can send them into negative spirals, so they avoid it for their own well-being.

Someone who is antisocial or doesn't like people will do what he or she wants and doesn't care about judgment. They actively disdain others and don't respect them. They may socialize, but there would be a clear reason and purpose for it, and once they have achieved it, they are done with you. That is not related to a social battery and is more related to a lack of empathy.

Introverts may appear unapproachable or arrogant because they are withdrawn and not proactively warm like many societies demand. They may have apathetic body language, missed smiles, and a lack of eye contact, but it's important to realize that it also describes someone who is about to fall asleep. As mentioned, introverts don't necessarily feel a certain way about themselves or evaluate themselves differently. You likely caught them just after what amounts to a social marathon for them, and they are trying to rest and recover—which can take hours to weeks.

Externally, there may not be much difference between a shy person, a socially awkward person, and an introvert, but you have to look past appearances to understand how they are different. The introvert just has a different operating system than extroverts.

If you've had a particular chatty week at work with little to no time alone, you might hermit yourself from Friday after work right to Monday morning. That sounds like a pretty fantastic weekend, doesn't it? You might even go through some extreme lengths to avoid talking to cashiers and baristas just because you feel the need to recharge yourself and fall into solitude.

A party full of people feels like a marathon to them, no matter how much they may have enjoyed themselves. Now, ask yourself this. Is it reasonable to ask someone to hit the gym *after* running a marathon? That's what asking an introvert to stay at a party after their battery is drained is like.

On the surface, an introvert may appear shy or even standoffish and uncomfortable—but that isn't because that's who they are. They're likely just tired, and their social batteries are exhausted for the time being. You saw them after they ran their marathon, and you got what was left. All they could muster was a smirk or nod of their head.

Extroverts are like a car that sits in the garage. If you don't start it up once every week, the fluids gum up and the pipes get clogged. Extroverts dislike alone time and become active and energetic from the presence of others.

Extroverts are the Energizer bunnies of society that simply can't get enough and never want the party to end. They're the first to show up and the last to leave, and they are generally bored with their own company. This doesn't make them dependent or weak; it just means they are stimulated by others.

Fortunately for extroverts, most Western societies place a premium on extroverted qualities. This is known as the *extrovert ideal* and is further propagated and reinforced by popular media. This ideal has tricked many people, including myself, into trying to be someone I'm not.

We correctly note that talkative children are doted on, and then we grow a bit more only to see that what attracts the opposite sex is something of a loud, brash personality. It's more of the same in the office, where your only option in job interviews is to describe yourself as "a people person" and "a great teammate." It's only a matter of time until we try to emulate the extrovert ideal in some way.

The key to being successful as an introvert is to know your limits and set your expectations. Remember that we are making the shift from chasing the extrovert ideal to finding the social rhythm that works for you as an introvert.

- Expect that you will hit a wall when it comes to social events.
- Expect that your calendar can feel overwhelming at times.
- Expect that regardless of whether you actually want to attend, you still want to be invited.
- Expect that you may take anywhere from hours to weeks to fully recover and feel social again.
- Expect that others won't understand you and will demand explanations from time to time.
- Expect that your relationships may change as a result of your need for time alone.
- Expect that the concept of what you find enjoyable will change.
- Expect that the extrovert ideal will continually be pushed on you.
- Expect to feel strange asserting and prioritizing your needs for alone time over other people.

To drive home the point of misused labels, let's take a look at some of history's most famous and successful introverts: Bill Gates, Abraham Lincoln, Albert Einstein, Mahatma Gandhi, Audrey Hepburn, Steve Jobs, and Warren Buffett.

Their sheer success indicates that they were not able to indulge in their introvert needs as often as they wanted to. Can you imagine Bill Gates needing to restrict contact with people and recharging for three days?

The key is that they all found clever and effective ways to work with their social batteries to accomplish whatever goals they set. That's the true focus on this book: how to optimize your social performance when you're exhausted and in need.

Introvert Defined

Introversion is one of the major personality traits studied in many psychological theories. The word *introvert* was used for the very first time, along with the word *extrovert*, during the 1920s when renowned psychologist Carl Jung published *Psychologische Typen*—or *Psychological Types,* as it's known in English.

According to Jung, introversion is a psychological mode wherein an individual considers his or her inner reality of utmost importance.

This means introverts tend to be more inward-focused, and they often retreat from the outside world to be able to focus their energy inward. They tend to be more focused on their internal thoughts and emotions rather than being engrossed in trying to find stimulation from the external environment. These individuals normally keep things to themselves and are defensive of the demands of the outside world. They are contemplative, cautious, and similar to a cat—sometimes the cat wants to play, and other times you can't get them out from their hiding spot under the bed.

How do we know if a person is an introvert? There are a number of traits introverts possess that can distinguish them as this personality type.

For one, introverts don't mind being alone—often, they prefer it. They are comfortable spending time by themselves and see it as a reprieve from the noisy world outside. They can easily entertain themselves by reading a book, watching a movie, or killing time with one-player games. If the introvert is a hiding cat, the extrovert is a golden retriever who wants to be petted all the time.

Introverts also find small talk a waste of time and energy. It exhausts their social battery faster than any other activity, and it seems to be all for nothing. Because of this, introverts are more likely to participate in deep and meaningful conversations. If they are going to expend their precious social energy, it may as well be for something that is significant or intimate. Nothing comes without a cost.

They like the *idea* of parties, family gatherings, and a night out with friends. However, participating in these events is a chore for them and they might be looked at with dread. Anticipation can be exciting, yet actual engagement is more typically exhausting.

Instead of going to bars or clubs, introverted individuals would rather cook dinner for a small group of friends. Rather than a poker night that lasts until 3:00 am, they would simply retire after work and watch basketball on television. They oftentimes would rather miss out on something than face social exhaustion.

Introverts can be confusing to understand. Outgoing individuals may find them difficult to understand because, to extroverts, if you like someone, you want to spend more time with them. It's important for the friends of introverts to gain an understanding of their nature so they don't take things personally when their attempts at socialization are rejected. Whatever the external actions of the introvert, it's about them, not you: they are practicing self-preservation and avoiding discomfort most of the time.

As such, it is very important to keep in mind the following:

- Respect their need for alone time and don't take it personally.
- Give them some time to adapt to new situations, because they are already uncomfortable.
- Don't jump to apathy or malice when introversion could be an explanation.

We meet introverts every day, and we have to learn how to create more harmonious relationships with them. If you identify as an introvert, understanding yourself better will help you connect and coexist with others. Acknowledging the fact that we are not all similar helps create a balance and also frees you from unfair expectations you may feel from a society at large.

We all have our own ways of getting by, and it is wrong to judge someone negatively just because they have feelings toward things. If you love chocolate, can you judge someone for loving vanilla instead?

Biological Differences

Because this is a book of actionable tactics, you are likely less interested in the true differences in brain chemistry between introverts and extroverts, so I'll leave you with one of the primary factors: baseline arousal.

The brain of an introvert has a higher level of baseline arousal; it's constantly busy and never turns off, as shown by multiple researchers including Hans Eysenck.

Think of the brain like a power generator. Suppose a power generator runs at a level of 500 watts while on standby, while another power generator runs at a level of 50 watts while on standby. Both of these power generators stop functioning at a level of 1000 watts.

The introvert is the power generator that runs at a background level of 500 watts, which means it is always active, alert, and analyzing.

However, it's also much closer to the limit of 1000 watts, which means it can more easily be overwhelmed, blow up, and shut down. In fact, it has to be careful of how much stimulation it gets, otherwise it just might shut down from external interference and overloading the circuits. For the introvert, this can be too much social interaction, conversation, or the presence of people in general.

Extroverts, on the other hand, can handle being surrounded by people and loud noises. They're only starting at 50 watts, after all. They don't need time to unplug and recharge alone after social interactions. Instead, they are only minimally stimulated, so they are actively seeking out highly stimulating environments to raise their arousal levels.

Another helpful analogy is to compare extroverts to a steel wall while introverts are a glass window. Obviously, it is going to take less impact to break the glass window, and thus, introverts are more sensitive because of their inherent build. Sometimes, we just can't help how we are wired.

It's clear how introverts have to pace themselves a bit more and make sure to keep their average usage rate lower because they are starting from a different point than extroverts are.

Chapter 2. Your Surprising Strengths

It's easy to sit back and marvel at an extroverted individual's seemingly superhuman powers in drawing energy into the wee hours of the morning. It's like they're energy vampires and only grow stronger as the people around them grow weaker, as if they utilize other people's presence for their sustenance. *How do they do that?*

Remember, they are literally operating with different brain chemistry, so don't feel too bad about not living up to those standards. After all, you've embodied that kind of energy in the past as well; however, it's more of the exception rather than the rule.

For a moment, let's imagine a party that only introverts ended up attending. It would start early, and people would be scattered around in tiny groups engrossed in substantial conversations about important issues. Then everyone's social battery would start to drain, they would grow annoyed with other people, and they'd start getting more sarcastic and acerbic. Then everyone would leave the party early and be home in time for their television shows.

Throw a few extroverts in there and you will get a dramatically different scene—for the context, dare I say *better*? Extroverts are amazing in many ways, but the grass isn't always greener and you shouldn't let your own unique strengths fall by the wayside. Remember that introverts *can* accomplish nearly everything an extrovert does, just not as frequently or consistently. In some cases, extroverts may never be able to do some of what we discuss in this chapter.

Disadvantages of the Extrovert

There is indeed an extrovert ideal that exists, as well as our innate feelings that life would be easier if we could throw ourselves into all the social situations we are invited to. It's a tempting thought, but it's basically another way of assuming that the grass is greener on the other side of the fence. Extroverts don't have life easy just because they thrive around people.

In fact, that's a pitfall in itself—as you may have learned in any other aspect of life, dependence on anything you can't yourself provide is risky at best. Extroverts can feel lonely and discontented by themselves, something that doesn't lend well to self-sufficiency and independence. They can indeed be seen as dependent, clingy, and high-maintenance as a friend or significant other, especially if they keep calling on the same group of people to socialize.

They can be exhausting and be the friend that never leaves and always overstays their welcome—only they don't know it. Suppose that you suddenly have a vacation and none of your friends can keep you company because they have to work—are you going to enjoy your vacation alone, or will it be energy-less and boring without company?

Extroverts suffer from the burden of other peoples' expectations. If you take a stereotypical view, extroverts are bundles of infectious energy, and sometimes people can come to depend on that from them. Yes, it can be a mutually beneficial dependency sometimes. But what about times that you don't feel it or you're just tired? Extroverts are expected to be perpetually upbeat and carry any conversation, which can create a certain amount of pressure and expectation. It's a burden to be *on* all the time.

It might be nice to be in the spotlight. However, spotlights get hot. Being the life of the party can also mean that you are carrying a big load: you're the one who has to keep the party going. That's a lot of responsibility. It can crush a lot of people, even when they've naturally taken on the role. It can be especially burdensome for someone who doesn't really have the personality for it.

To be an extrovert, you have to be a self-sustaining star and source of social energy. Others take from you, and you provide for others. This means that you have to put out a lot of energy in order to get a small amount of returns.

Extroverts also suffer from the pressure of their own expectations. People are *supposed* to like you, and you are *supposed* to get along great with people and in groups. They have the expectation to perform well socially.

Well, what if they *don't* like you? There's no telling if you have somehow become "that guy" or "that girl" that talks and talks without any semblance of self-awareness. You're continually alienating your energy source, and that's a very scary proposition. You might be the center of attention, but it could be for precisely the wrong reasons. Will you still seek out people's attention, even if it's not because they think highly of you? What would your alternative be?

You might imagine this is troublesome, especially if combined with the tendency of extroverts to want to simply engage, and engaging also leads to them frequently violating boundaries of other people. If you play with an excited puppy for a while who was happy to see you, it might just prod you too much and cross the line into being annoying or even make a mess on your carpet (not that I'm comparing extroverts to dogs, but it's an apt analogy).

This entire section is a longwinded way giving the perspective that being an introvert is not so bad.

Introverts don't have the problem of being dependent on others and will rarely become "that guy" or "that girl" because they simply won't hang around long enough to get on anyone's nerves. If it's boring small talk to an extrovert, then it's soul-crushing and excruciating to the introvert. They'll engage for as long as they need to and then get out. If it was up to them, they'd rather not be there anyway. As a result, you also won't find introverts violating boundaries as often as their extrovert counterparts.

Of course, that can be taken negatively as well. They're socially low-maintenance, sometimes to a fault. Here's how a phone call ends with an introvert: "Got it? Okay, bye [click]."

There are no inherent expectations that you will show up to a party, captivate people, and otherwise be a dancing monkey to help entertain others. People invite you because they enjoy your company, not because of the social atmosphere you might create. Introverts are likely to be more motivated to leave, so there are also no internal expectations to perform well and psych themselves out.

Finally, introverts just might have a more accurate view of their social circle. They tend to engage with far fewer people in general and prefer quality time over quantity and breadth. They know who they like and who they want to spend time with. This can often be counted on one hand. They are okay with keeping others are arm's lengths or just leaving them as acquaintances.

Overall, it's a balance.

Immunity to Boredom

Recall that introverts, by definition, draw energy from their alone time, and being around others isn't typically their preferred idea of enjoyment. This means they are supremely independent and even prefer solo activities.

They have a tendency to entertain themselves because they are usually happier that way. Where an extrovert needs people and events to be stimulated, an introvert can be stimulated in just about any setting, especially one where only they exist. One relies on others, one is self-sufficient.

What's fun for each personality type? Well, one definition involves relying on others, and the other does not.

Because they don't necessarily need others for entertainment, this creates a relative immunity to boredom. They've always got something to do or think about and aren't dependent on others to keep them entertained, give them energy, or organize an activity. When they are tired, they can simply retreat and recharge themselves, which is another push toward self-sufficiency and convenience. After all, it's easier to avoid people than to spend time with them, isn't it? If you compare energy sources, the introvert's is infinite and easy to find, whereas the extrovert's is much less so.

Introverts can make for extremely low-maintenance friends if you don't mind the fact that they can sometimes be *absentee* friends to satisfy their own needs. Again, this can work against them because introverts can be self-sufficient to a fault, which results in hermitdom occasionally. Overall, it's pretty neat to realize that you are essentially never bored—except of certain people.

Introspection and Observation

Introverts tend to be inside their own heads just a tad more frequently. It's not necessarily a sign of intelligence or increased mental horsepower; it just means there is more attention paid to small things that you can only get from observation, as opposed to actively participating on your environment. It comes down to the fact that when you listen instead of talk, you are in a position of collecting information as opposed to disseminating it.

For some introverts, their inner monologue is something they wish they could turn on and off—but that's the basis of this strength. Introverts have the tendency to think, overthink, reflect, and adapt to situations better than extroverts because they are more likely to be processing rather than expressing.

It's part of the reason they may speak up less

frequently: they are thinking about what to say, and they are measuring the words and their impact before they tumble out of their mouths. They take the totality of their message into account, such as their facial expressions, tone of voice, body language, and the possible implications and assumptions of what they're saying.

This might be helpful toward problem-solving and analyzing risk in situations. Thoughtfulness also allows you to correct errors far more easily than others. When they deviate or make a mistake, they can pinpoint where it occurred and prevent the error from happening again. There is an element of natural cautiousness—after all, isn't the introvert's main motivation to avoid situations of social discomfort? Introverts are simply more likely to be thinking about themselves, their environments, and anything else aside from the actual conversation at hand. To reiterate, this says nothing about how accurate or insightful they might be, but the more attention and time you spend on something, you might have a better chance of accuracy and insight.

Self-reflection and thoughtfulness are one of the introvert's greatest powers. It can also mean that they are more sensitive to stimuli, patterns, and behavior of others—which is great for reading people and even leading them.

Deep Work

On a related note, if introverts are so observant and analytical, it means they might have a proclivity toward deep, uninterrupted work.

Introverts have the tendency to be alone and seek solitude—sounds like a setting that is conducive to immense productivity. They don't tolerate the most distracting of distractions in people. In fact, they occasionally avoid them like the plague. If you think about it, an empty room with a task to keep them busy and no one around has all of the aspects of an environment that an introvert might feel most comfortable in. As an introvert, you probably also have a great ability to concentrate well and process large amounts of information. That means that you can prepare better than others and that you can be better informed and make creative connections that others don't see. Being able to concentrate well also brings the ability to pay attention to detail. Seeing details that others don't see gives you an opportunity to really have an impact when you say something or you can mitigate risks much better.

Group work? It can be more productive and efficient, but it's also something else for the introvert to worry about and contribute to their fatigue.

This penchant for solitude can lead to the introvert intentionally plugging away in the midst of chaos, actually using work to procrastinate or avoid being cornered in a cubicle and having their ears talked off. They don't require the spotlight and are content to work behind the scenes and remain undistracted. Their emotional needs are not being starved by being away from others, so they will keep on working.

Taken to the extreme, this results in someone who focuses on work to their detriment, where they avoid office politicking and don't cultivate important relationships. As always, moderation is important, but it can never be a negative to be someone who constantly positions themselves for massive productivity.

Increased solitude and separation are likely to be the norm in terms of employment, if not completely remote and "out of office" arrangements. In other words, the world is trending in a way that coworkers, if you even have them, may not be physically present. The evolution of technology favors introverts.

Deep Bonds

You may have heard the oft-repeated phrase that introverts are great listeners.

It's likely to be true, but not for the reason

44

that is usually put forth. Introverts are great listeners because it's a lower drain on their social batteries than talking and engaging actively. In essence, listening is easier to do for longer periods of time for them. It's passive—they ask questions and listen to the answers because it's easier than telling stories about themselves. Introverts listen well in part not because they care more; they just speak less, which makes others speak more. However, this does necessarily mean that you are listening better and more in tune with what people are communicating, consciously or subconsciously.

Second, introverts are great listeners because when people are allowed to speak, they are allowed to show their interesting sides. Where you might hear a story about someone's mundane weekend in one instance, the introvert might be able to hear just why they almost broke both of their legs that weekend.

This, of course, creates a self-perpetuating cycle: the more you allow someone to speak, the more interesting they are, the more you care, and the more you want them to speak. When you're curious about someone or something, you want to learn what you can about them, and you're completely content if the focus is not on you.

Another dynamic that occurs with introverts is the tendency to engage only one or a few people at once. Large parties aren't preferable as they are unnecessarily draining and taxing, but small gatherings are tolerable and worthwhile pursuits. In such an environment, it is much easier to get to know people on a deeper, more personal level.

Some might also contend that introverts tend to create deeper bonds because they abhor small talk and shallow conversation. It drains their social battery without a tangible purpose, so it just serves to bring them discomfort. Thus, they want to have meaningful conversations and discuss real topics with emotional ramifications. This type of conversation might also be draining, but introverts can feel that it's worth it because at least there is a very real payoff.

If introverts prefer to focus on small groups of people and deep conversation, then deep bonds are a natural consequence and can form easily. This is not to say that extroverts cannot also do the same, but they may be more inclined to mindless chatter just to fill the silence.

Summon the Inner Extrovert

Here's the thing. As you well know, even though you are innately X, Y, and Z by nature, it doesn't mean you can't throw off your introvert shackles and channel your inner extrovert when needed. We've all had instances where we felt like the life of the party and could banter endlessly with others.

It's not just a matter of trying to be someone you're not. In all walks of life, if we act like someone we're not, it leaves us with a sinking feeling. It is doubly so with manipulating your social battery. Extroverts trying to be introverts become listless and lonely, while introverts trying to be extroverts become exhausted and frustrated.

So what brings these rare events on? There are two subtle mindset shifts you can utilize to rearrange your mental furniture and project extroverted traits on command.

First, try to be less self-conscious.

Self-consciousness is the key to self-sabotage. When you can't stop thinking about how you will be perceived, it becomes impossible to communicate your thoughts clearly. Remember the primary biological difference between introvert and extrovert brains—the baseline levels of arousal? This is where it actually affects you in a negative sense.

When introverts speak, listen, or react, they're always checking multiple dials and dashboards. They're monitoring themselves and trying to take a step back and survey the entire conversation and situation. That's part of why being an introvert is so exhausting. You live inside your head while the world revolves around you, and you can't shut off the parts of your brain that run background processes, sapping your social battery.

Introvert also tend to be self-conscious about their social battery. Introverts know themselves. They know they have only a certain amount of social energy to play with. This is why they may have a lot of anxiety in social settings—not because people make them uneasy and not because social interactions threaten or frighten them. It is because they know what will happen when their social energy runs out.

The problem with having self-consciousness as a problem is the more you focus on it, the more self-conscious you become and the worse your mistakes get. It's like commanding someone to not think about elephants—what do you suppose might immediately appear in their mind?

Easier said than done, but attempting to clear your mind and proactively shut off your background processes will help you extrovert on command. One way to start is by turning your attention away from your inner self and focusing on the person in front of you—by being present, so to speak. Get lost in their words, stories, and presence.

We might be so caught up in self-monitoring that you don't allow yourself to feel interested or curious because you are more concerned that you might be soon drained of social energy. Real curiosity is one of the easiest ways to wipe out self-consciousness, because you literally forget about it in that moment.

Remember how you felt about whatever your new monthly obsession was as a child? For me, it was dinosaurs, and you could not have shut me up about them. If I had an inkling that you knew anything about dinosaurs, I would have peppered you with questions until my parents forced me into bed.

It's similar to why many people enjoy playing sports for fitness versus just toiling away in the gym. When you can lose yourself in the moment of running and jumping, you enjoy the activity because you forget about the fitness aspect of it all. The self-consciousness gives way to a stronger motivation.

The more you enjoy yourself, the less self-conscious you become and the longer your social battery keeps its charge.

The second way to summon your inner extrovert is to attempt to be less judgmental.

All the signs are there for introverts to be more judgmental, if you are being honest with yourself. They are routinely characterized as inward-focused, analytical, and more reserved. Additionally, they grow sick and tired of people easily because their social battery runs low, but also likely because they think people aren't worth growing fatigued for.

Like it or not, introverts have the tendency to be judgmental, picky, and not give the benefit of the doubt. It's usually a negative trait, regardless of whether you are mostly correct or not. You are quick to impose judgment on someone based on little to no information about them. You are making judgments based on assumptions and imperfect information. You are making judgments based on the tip of the iceberg and one moment in time that probably isn't representative of them as a person.

If you identify as an introvert, you might find it hard to deny this point. When introverts are judgmental, it usually means they see the worst in others. They don't give regard for circumstance, context, or reason.

What effect does all of this negative ideation have? Whatever you think tends to become true to you.

Because they've shoved people into a predefined box, their expectations about others are dramatically lowered. It's a result of staying inside your head and observing situations more than participating in them. Subsequently, you will be compelled to withdraw if you feel like *someone isn't good enough for you.*

Be honest: do you feel like people aren't good enough for you, entertaining, amusing, interesting, smart, or worth your time?

It's sapping your ability to extrovert on command because you simply won't care. And it also creates a self-fulfilling prophecy, wherein you treat them like they're boring, so you ask them boring questions that reward you with boring answers.

If you can curtail this need for judgment and self-consciousness, you'll be able to realize the unique, counterintuitive strengths you have simply because you grow tired of people easily. You'll see it's not necessarily even a weakness, just a different approach to social situations.

Chapter 3. Extend Your Social Battery

When you get down to it, there is not much difference between introverts and other temperaments besides how their social batteries become depleted.

However, this seemingly small aspect greatly affects how people view the situations they come across. Things can be exciting or anxiety-inducing, interesting or not worth the trouble, enjoyable or exhausting. It's not a stretch to say that the actions of introverts are dictated by their social batteries in much the same way that a thorn dictates what a huge lion does.

It's rarely convenient for the introvert to lock themselves in their room to recharge, depending on the myriad of obligations and duties we all have on a daily basis. Once you reach that critical level of social fatigue, what can you do? Most of the time, not much besides try to stretch that fake smile across your face and end up looking like a psychopath surveying their prey. This is when your friends will ask you why you're so grumpy for no apparent reason.

Therefore, this chapter is focused on not only extending your social battery, but also preserving it and putting yourself in situations where you don't have to rely on it as much.

Think of it like an extra battery pack you carry to keep your social battery around 50 percent charged—because once it drops below 10 percent, there's no coming back unless you do a true charging period of solitude. We know that you can gab with the best, but you may not get the opportunity to showcase your skills because you are perpetually too tired.

Silent Reactions

Using *silent reactions* is going to shift the focus from your mental faculties to your facial muscles, which can reduce the burden on your social battery.

When we talk to people, reactions are a big part of the conversation—a much larger part than you probably realize. When you're talking, you're actively participating, but you should also be actively participating while listening through properly reacting to people's words. Unfortunately, listening is not a passive activity. To speak to someone without reactions would be like speaking to a brick wall. You have no indication if anything vibrated their eardrums and made any type of impact.

Reactions are first and foremost an acknowledgment that you heard what someone said and you are processing it. Most reactions people use are verbal, and sometimes we use questions as reactions. This is tiring and isn't easy on your social battery.

Get into the habit of giving silent reactions, which are reactions with your body language, facial expressions, and noises you make with your mouth that aren't words. Pretend that you are mute and can only respond nonverbally, and that will give you an idea of how to start with this.

In reacting, silently or otherwise, the goal is to acknowledge them and make them feel heard and validated. You can do this most effectively by attempting to isolate the primary emotion the other person is trying to convey and by *showing that to them*. If someone has a story about wrecking their car, you would nonverbally show them sadness and dismay. If someone has a story about getting scolded by a clown, you would show them amusement and incredulity.

There actually aren't that many emotions to react to when people tell us stories or share about themselves. It's usually some mixture of surprise, shock, humor, sadness, amusement, or amazement.

This works beautifully because it's a little bit easier to raise an eyebrow and wave your hands about than to formulate responses and reply to people. This is relatively self-explanatory with body language and facial expressions, even if the facial expressions are a bit strained and forced—it's still less taxing.

What about non-word noises?

These include, for example, *"Hmm"* or *"Mmm"* with a flat tone, a rising tone, a lowering tone, and varying length and inflection. These can get across a whole lot in just a simple sound and can replace entire sentences. Some of these non-words can be questions, statements, and even opinions. Get better at substituting full sentences or questions with these non-word noises and you'll be able to have the same range of expressiveness either way.

For example, "Do you like mangos?"

"Mm," in a dismissive tone would clearly signal "No" while a longer, drawn-out "Mmm…" might signal "Yes, sometimes…"
"Mmm?" might signal "What in the world are you talking about?"
"Mm…" in a sing-songy tone might indicate "Yes, I can't live without them."

These are the least battery-draining responses because it's just a rumble in your throat with a specific tone, perhaps paired with a look in your eye that can replace sentences upon sentences. In terms of energy expenditure, you can't beat these, and your social battery will thank you for it.

Question Master

As the previous point mentioned, the part about social interactions that drains your social battery is really responding and providing your own material—such as telling a story or just talking about your day.

Asking questions of other people ranks far, far lower on how it drains your social battery. It represents a more passive role versus active role in answering questions. Think about a job interview and how much more the interviewee is expected to talk and feels the pressure—you should strive to be on the more relaxed side of the interviewer.

In other words, to make conversations less effort, turn into the question master. People enjoy talking about themselves and what interests them, so if you can ask questions that convey your interest in them, you will be set for a while.

When's the last time you asked someone five questions in a row? Does that feel weird or uncomfortable? If you mentally answered yes, you clearly don't ask many questions and are putting yourself into the active role in a conversation of answering questions.

Here is my suggestion for extending your social battery. No matter how the other person replies, you will ask them four questions. Then, after the four questions, share something about yourself. There's essentially a ratio of four to one of talking about the other person to talking about yourself. Even if you know you should ask more questions, sometimes it can be hard to think of what to ask, effectively fatiguing you and undermining the whole thing. So instead of struggling with that on the fly, here's an effective template of sorts for asking more effective questions.

Specific question
Specific question
Broad question
Broad question

Specific questions are about specific details and components of a topic. If you're talking about tables, specific questions would be where you bought it, how much it cost, what the material is, why you bought this particular table, or who paid for it. You are asking for distinct pieces of information and facts.

Broad questions are when you zoom out on a

topic and try to understand the context around it. If you're talking about tables, broad questions would be the motivation for a new table, home décor, the thought process, or why the old table was inadequate. You are asking for thoughts and reasons as opposed to information and facts.

You don't have to use this template, but it does behoove you to ask more questions and occasionally put more pressure and conversational burden on other people.

Use Short Bursts

I like to call this the *blitzkrieg* approach.

The truth is, if you are forced to interact with someone for an undefined period of time, that can feel as daunting as looking up at Mount Everest. (By the way, this is why small talk in an elevator or a short grocery store line isn't so bad—because we can see a defined point for escaping.)

Who knows if you're going to be interested in

this person or if they are a good conversationalist themselves, not even mentioning how tiring it's going to be for you? It's an investment and is definitely going to drain your social battery.

Instead of giving a lukewarm effort for 60 minutes, focus on giving a short burst of 20 minutes of extreme engagement and interest in the other person. Then excuse yourself and use the rest of the 20 minutes to recharge and find solitude. Those 20 intense minutes will drain your social battery roughly the same amount as having to pretend to care and smile for an hour, so you might as well use that energy for something good.

In the worst-case scenario, you'll save yourself 40 minutes and simply be over with it sooner rather than later. In the best-case scenario, you just might find that you actually enjoy the other person, and this intense engagement mode you're in could provide a serious amount of rapport and bonding.

If you find that you can't quite cut something

down to 20 minutes, you can strategically schedule activities to interrupt talking, like watching a video or taking a walk, so you at least don't have to persevere for 60 minutes straight.

Dealing with Small Talk

The vast majority of introverts have a love-hate relationship with small talk—well, mostly hate.

We begrudgingly recognize that small talk is often the path to real relationships. The way that you might start talking to and connect with your future best friend is probably through a combination of small talk and luck. No matter whom we meet, it's usually the gatekeeper that we have to get past to connect with people on a deeper level.

Most of the purpose of small talk is to aim for the lowest common denominator, the lowest hanging fruit. You want to shoot for something that everyone can relate to, and that's why there is so much information flying around about the weather, the traffic, the latest viral video, and pop culture events.

However, author Laurie Helgoe put it best by stating, "We hate small talk because we hate the barrier it creates between people." Small talk allows us to have entire conversations where people speak a lot without saying anything. In other words, it just serves to fill the silence and it's how we go through the motions of social courtesy.

When small talk is left unattended and to its own devices, it usually degenerates into empty babble like the weather. Small talk becomes just that: small. It is shallow, superficial chatter and a waste of the precious social battery.

Of course, it doesn't have to be that. Instead of dancing from shallow topic to shallow topic as you're accustomed to, just bypass it. Skip it and go straight to what's important or interesting to you. The best way to deal with small talk (for everyone, really) is to simply opt out of it and try to build a real bond with people.

Instead of asking about the weather, ask how someone feels about the pending political situation. Instead of asking about the traffic, ask about someone's worldview in relation to their occupation. Instead of asking about how someone's weekend was, ask someone what their most embarrassing moment was. These questions don't break the ice—they skip that part of the conversation because it doesn't need to exist. There don't need to be courtesy questions about someone's background before diving into what they actually think and feel.

To deal best with small talk, avoid it completely and dive into meaningful topics and questions. If you are courteous and seem genuinely curious and nonjudgmental, the only boundaries you will be violating are in your own head.

To continue with this trend, make it your goal to go *deep*. The problem with wide-ranging and expansive discussions is they are necessarily shallow. In practical terms, this means to stay on only a few topics at a time and go deeper within them. Narrow your field of inquiry and aim for an inch wide and a mile deep.

Key phrases:

1. Why?
2. Tell me more about that.
3. What was the thinking/motivation/intention behind that?
4. That reminds me of a time in my life...
5. How did that impact your life?
6. Can you elaborate more on that?
7. Tell me the origin of that story!
8. How did that make you feel?

See how you're going beyond the regular *who, what, when, where, and why*? You're focusing on the emotions that people feel and the consequences of the actions in their lives.

You can also strive to go deeper through consciously pushing the envelope into the territory of *inappropriate*. When you're more open to what you discuss with people, and can feel comfortable veering into the slightly inappropriate, people will immediately warm to you because you've treated them with familiarity rather than like a stranger.

What topics do you talk to your friends about? Think back to the last few conversations you had with a close friend. Now contrast that with a conversation you might have with a stranger you meet at a networking event. You probably felt a need to stay *safe* to avoid judgment or offending them. But which was more interesting and enjoyable? The deeper, so-called inappropriate conversation, hands down.

Distract Yourself

Another way to phrase this section would be to treat yourself like a child. What do you do when you have to give a child a shot with a huge needle? You distract him or her with a clown or corgi.

In essence, a good method to extend your

social battery is to distract yourself with a *goal*. For example: I like going to the beach on occasion, but I don't like staying there for extended periods of time. Lying idly in the sun just isn't my idea of an ideal day.

I like the sun and the water, but the part about the beach I don't like is that it feels like there is no purpose to it. People go to the beach just because it's the beach. Now, on the other hand, I'd be thrilled to go to the beach to play volleyball or to catch an amazing sunset view. I would have a clear reason to be there and it would make it more fulfilling for me. It would actually make me excited about it and not just counting down the minutes until I leave.

Most introverts view socializing like I view the beach. A lot of the time, there's no focus or purpose to it, and that makes it something that we want to avoid. Socializing for socializing's sake isn't something that we're interested in because we know it's just going to drain us and possibly put us in an uncomfortable position. We're tired after playing volleyball, but we don't notice it until afterward and it doesn't disturb our day.

So distract yourself with a social goal. If you have an overarching goal or purpose to drive you to continue your social interactions, oftentimes that can serve to push you past the limitations of your social battery charge.

Let me give you another example. Suppose that your social battery was exhausted because you had a four-hour meeting every day at work that week. You're spent and you just want to go home and hide under the covers for about 20 hours. But your car breaks down on the way back, and the only way you can escape your situation is to flag down another car and charm them into letting you use their phone and tire iron. It would require no small amount of small talk and social interaction, especially if they give you a ride to the nearest gas station.

Would interacting socially be a problem in that situation? No, because you had an overarching goal that made everything else essentially irrelevant. Your goal of fixing you car vetoed your social exhaustion. You had something you needed to accomplish, and you were able to push through to it no matter how tired you were.

That's the power of having a social goal.

If you dread networking events (and we all do on some level), then what is a social goal you can use to accomplish something rather than going just to do some open-ended networking? The goals for a networking event are clearer than most because you are looking to either benefit your personal career or your company. If your company is truly strapped for cash or you are desperate to find a new job, that social goal can help you push through being socially exhausted and meeting a few more people than you would otherwise.

Social goals take your mind off your social expenditure and give you something that matters more for the moment. Instead of conversations becoming freewheeling, open-ended social exercises, you have a clear idea as to the kind of objectives you want to walk away with, and you can focus all your efforts toward that. It's also a question of motivation—your desire and drive toward that end goal can be a greater motivator to stay and "tough it out" as opposed to scurrying away with our tails in between our legs.

We are, after all, creatures of pleasure. We tend to run away from pain and toward pleasure. With the process of setting up-front goals that will focus your social efforts, you may not be able to increase the pleasure you get from extended social interaction, but you will be able to decrease the associated pain, which is powerful.

Compete against others or yourself. Instead of listlessly wandering during a networking event, what if you set a goal for yourself to collect as many business cards as possible or to learn the middle names of four people at the event? Other examples would be learning everyone's first name and place of birth at a party, verbally maneuvering an opening to tell that one story of yours to at least two different people, successfully getting some fresh air outside with two separate people, exchanging social media accounts with three people, or learning an embarrassing story about four people that night.

Sherlock Holmes, the famous literary detective, would use his powerful skills of deduction through asking questions and making observations. You can make it your goal to learn as much about other people, make observations about them, and put them all together in a few assumptions about them.

Ask as many questions as you can, ask about your observations, and test your assumptions by asking them about those. Use your sense of curiosity and try to find what's interesting about people you meet.

Goals can keep you entertained by an ulterior motive and generally keep you invested in other people. That's really the underlying purpose—to care more about others than your fatigue.

Use Solitude Effectively

Finding your quiet time and solitude, of course, is how you will preserve your social battery the most. Most other techniques just make it drain a little less slowly.

Make sure that you (1) get your alone time and (2) use it in a way that will allow you to actually recharge.

The first step is planning for it on a daily basis. You might be surprised as to how much better you feel the next day if you get your daily solitude. Some might need it only on a weekly basis; and others might need it at lunch and before bedtime just to get through the day. Some of us like to eat six small meals a day, and others eat only a huge dinner and nothing else the rest of the day. If you're constantly moody or irritable, try blocking off time for solitude in your schedule on a daily basis. Set hard barriers for others to abide by, and put these blocked-off times into your calendar first—force yourself and others to plan around it and make them priorities. Treat it as strictly as you might schedule a work meeting or gym session.

Next, we know that we need solitude, but what is the actual act of solitude? Do we just need to sit in a room with the lights turned off and ice cream in our mouth?

Do what relaxes you, and don't do what others say you should do to relax (including me). Everyone has a different idea of what they want to come home to after a long, chatty day. Some might not even want to go home—perhaps they want to go to a jazz bar with a drink in hand.

How do you prefer all of your five senses to be stimulated? Do they contribute to your sense of solitude and recharging? Do you prefer to do something with your hands to feel productive? Does your mental exhaustion contribute to actual physical exhaustion, or would a gym session invigorate you? Does physical activity soothe you and de-stress you? Is social media helpful or actually detrimental to your sense of solitude and relaxation? Is talking to people online or on your phone draining or comforting? Should you ditch your phone and unplug (it) to recharge (yourself)?

Everyone is different, but what is universal is that solitude is something to embrace. It's not rest, which can be taken in a multitude of negative ways. Don't feel guilty about taking a break or not being productive for a change. It's recovery, which is something professional athletes do between training and competition. It's something you are entitled to, shouldn't feel ashamed about, and ultimately need.

Grow Your Social Battery

Probably the most effective way at dealing with fatiguing social situations is to simply have a bigger social battery. Grow it yourself and you may never find that you are hovering around 10 percent.

To grow your social battery, you must exercise it. And to exercise it, you must deliberately leave your comfort zone and push your limits. Yes, it's annoying and frustrating, but the social battery, in addition to functioning like a battery, also functions like a muscle. The more you work at it, the stronger and more resilient it will become; if you neglect it, it will wither and atrophy correspondingly.

Leaving your social comfort zone starts with not hiding in your bathroom like a cat at every potential interaction. Start to say yes more, or even adopt a "Never say no" policy regarding social events. You can also try some of the following:

- Engage someone in a grocery store line.
- Leave your house every day (not including work) for at least an hour.
- Be the first one to a party.
- Be the last one to leave a party.
- Ask a barista or cashier at least four questions.
- Plan something for your group of friends at least once a week.

It's almost as if you are living someone else's life, isn't it? A resilient social battery is necessary to live your best life, so perhaps it's time to inject a little bit of change for once.

Chapter 4. Introvert Life Design

One of the biggest nightmares for an introvert is mandatory socializing.

This can take many forms. The most common one is probably the dreaded industry networking event. You might have been asked to go by your supervisor, you face pressure from your coworkers, you feel like you need to show your face, or you feel essentially coerced into it because "it will be good for your career."

Whatever the reason, you're there after work when you're already tired. You're faced with other people that seem just as apathetic to the situation as you or people who refuse to leave you alone despite all of your signs that say otherwise.

Other forms of mandatory socializing occur at times that most other people can't seem to get enough of—holidays. For example, birthdays, Halloween, St. Patrick's Day, Thanksgiving, Christmas, and New Year's Eve. These are all times of expected and even obligatory socialization in large groups, most of the people in which you probably don't know. You might not prefer these occasions, but these are times where it's expected that you truly socialize.

These are excuses for parties, and introverts prefer to pick their parties selectively. We know that we don't want to engage in loud situations with strangers and no ending time in sight, but in what way can introverts actually socialize without being afraid of feeling exhausted or annoyed?

How can we design our lives and consistently

put ourselves into positions where we can feel comfortable and thrive instead of live in dread and anxiety? If you're comfortable in your surroundings, you will feel closer to your version of the extrovert ideal. If you're continually thinking of your exit plan versus focusing on the person in front of you, this will obviously impact your social performance.

Let's take a look at what you should consider in selecting your social battlefield.

Categorize Stimulation

In designing your life's interactions, you first have to understand the different types of social interactions there are and how they might affect your social battery. Some of these immediately sound off-putting and like a nightmare to you, while others you might think, "Yeah, I could do that frequently." Obviously, the goal is to skew your life toward more of the latter situations.

For our purposes, I want to put social interactions into four main categories, from most dreaded to most desired.

First: lots of strangers. These are what we typically hate because there is so much uncertainty and background chatter. It's tough to focus on one person because there is so much going on. Of course, these are networking events, huge parties, and music festivals where you aren't excited about the musical acts. Plainly put, these are nightmares that you try to avoid every time but aren't always able to do so. They are exhausting and can cause you to withdraw for days afterward. You might not even make it all the way through and just leave in the middle of any of these. Tolerance: 2–4 hours.

Second: lots of familiar faces. This differs from the first category because even though there are many people, you know or at least recognize almost all of them. These are still tiring, but nowhere near as tiring as having to break down barriers with each new stranger. Some of these faces might be annoying and fatiguing, but others will likely be sources of comfort and refuge. Friends or not, it's just a lot of stimulation and you'll still be exhausted by the end of it. This can even be your birthday party or weekend skiing trip, where you handpicked every single person. Tolerance: 3–5 hours.

Third: daily life. This is a variable category and can reach across all four categories. But most of the time, it's simply the amount of interaction you get from your job, school, buying things, intermittent chatting, and meeting with friends. If you stop to have a chat with a barista or cashier a few times a day, you might be more tired than usual, but you'll still have to get through class, a work meeting, and chatting with a professor. Sometimes you'll be able to stick to a routine where nothing drains you. All these seemingly small things take up bits of your social battery. Your state of mind and general state of fatigue or energy also affect how daily life affects you. In any case, you'll constantly be draining slowly. Tolerance: 8–12 hours.

Fourth: immune people. Everyone has safe people whom they actually don't really drain with and whom they feel absolute safety with. For some, this will be their significant others. For others, this will be a small handful of family or friends. Some might only have one person in this category! What makes these people immune is a certain threshold of comfort and the fact that we feel they accept our introverted tendencies. They seem to understand us and our nature and don't demand that we are any other way but ourselves. Whether it's them or us, they don't drain us. Tolerance: almost infinite.

So it's time to ask yourself who falls into these categories and what kinds of events you have been attending all this time. Take a moment to dissect your life and place people where they need to be for your own sanity. When you know the quantities of people and events you are dealing with, you can better design your life around conserving your energy and never growing what might be deemed *the irritating of the introvert.*

Predictability

You may not have realized it, but one of the aspects of random or obligatory socialization that introverts hate is the unpredictability of it all.

Events or activities that are open-ended, or that you have no knowledge about, scare the dickens out of you because, well, how long is your battery going to last, and when will you be able to recharge it?

For example, bar hopping—going with a group of people from bar to bar. Extroverts love this because the more bars they go to, the more different people they can engage with. There is action and movement, which energizes them.

The problem with socializing this way for introverts is that mixing with people and environments in unfamiliar territory requires untold amounts of social effort and attention. It's like you need to be at maximum alert to process and comprehend everything going on around you.

When you go to these places, you don't know who will be there. You don't know if there is an agenda. And even if there is an agenda, you don't know how it can deviate and take a turn for something you are wholly unprepared for.

Therefore, one of the keys to designing your life is to focus on predictability. Think about the *who, what, when, where, and why*. Insist on knowing these things before you head out to any event, and be intimately aware of these when you plan events for yourself. It's okay to have a little variation, but at least make sure it's variation you have accounted for! Remember, you're not actively controlling situations—you're simply filtering and understanding what you're up against.

Where: Focus on locations and settings that you know you will be comfortable in and where you know there will be few surprises. This speaks to venues and restaurants that you already know or are quiet and calm versus loud and animated. Will you be able to have a decent conversation, or is the venue conducive only to salsa dancing?

Who: Know who you will be spending time with and try to restrict the number of people to your close circle so you don't get overwhelmed talking to large groups. Restrict your socialization to just one or two strangers at a time—any more than that will be too tiring for you. Are the people coming chatterboxes, and if so, how many? Will there be people present who understand your nature and can indulge in it? Try to avoid people who spontaneously proclaim, "Hey, it's okay if I invite eight more people, right?"

When: This isn't a point about being punctual; rather, it's a point about having defined beginning and ending times. This puts a limit on the expenditure on your social battery. The most important part of this is to know exactly what you're getting yourself into time-wise and to give yourself a solid time to leave. You may not be able to count on yourself for leaving at a certain time, but if the event ends, then that can help you out. Keep it close-ended and nonnegotiable. It's for your own good.

What: This can tie neatly into the previous section about the categories of stimulation. What is the purpose of the event, what is the normal type of behavior there, and how will you be expected to act? Is the energy expenditure worth the payoff?

As mentioned, we don't mind talking while we are waiting in a grocery line or in an elevator, because we know these have defined ending points where we can escape. Keep the same in mind for your social events and occasions—know exactly how long they will be and when you will leave. It's impossible to understand every single scenario possible, but if you can prepare yourself with alternative options, your stress will decrease because you won't feel trapped and like you have no choice but to be incredibly uncomfortable.

By chasing predictability, you make sure you are prepared for what's to come and have the proper expectations about an event or hangout *before* you get there. You can do this by asking many thorough questions, most of which are designed to help you gauge just how socially exhausting something will be.

In essence, play a game of "Twenty Questions" before agreeing to anything social and you will be much happier with your friends.

For example, if a friend were to invite me to "a small party," I might show up and find that his definition of "small" is 40 people, none of whom I know. I would be annoyed at myself for not having more information beforehand and trying to determine if the social cost is worth the social benefit.

It's up to you to perform your due diligence before a social outing. Get as much information as possible so you can truly determine if you're up for it, if you can *get up* for it, and if you'll enjoy it.

Questions to ask:
• When does it start and end?

- Who is going?
- How many people are going?
- Who will I know there?
- What's the occasion?
- Where will it be?
- How do I get there?
- Will there be loud music?

Knowing the answers to these questions will allow you to pace yourself for the night or just opt out.

Plan Around Interests

What are your favorite activities, whether they involve people or not?

You might be comfortable sitting at a café or hanging out at a park, or taking long walks might set you at ease. Bike trips, hiking, or camping with a few close friends might be your thing. Or you might enjoy simply sitting at home on your couch and watching movies. Maybe you spend most of your free time either at the gym or training for a marathon.

These are your interests—plan around them. Engage people on *your* level, and invite them into your world and where you are comfortable. Instead of trying to conform to other people's setups and having to accommodate them, make them accommodate you. Planning around your interests keeps you in your comfort zone while inviting others to share it.

This is not in a sneaky or demanding manner; it just means that introverts should ideally be the planner and progenitor of their social events so they can control what's involved and how comfortable they will be. Become a more proactive planner and occupy that role in your group of friends.

If you're comfortable, you'll feel more open and relaxed, and that's not a situation that makes your social battery drain. Staying within your interests allows your social battery to run off reserves, because it doesn't have to deal with anything new, and you can focus on the task at hand. Try to keep those feelings of comfort in mind when you're in uncomfortable, novel situations.

Plan Around Expenditure

If you're like most people, you probably plan your schedule and calendar around your availability. For example, if you're free both Saturday afternoon and evening, then you would fill it with two activities. You're not taking anything into consideration other than how many hours you have free that are not accounted for.

This is not a smart thing for introverts to do.

Introverts should plan around *energy expenditure*. Let's assume that an introvert has 100 energy units a day. How will you use them to your greatest benefit? Suppose that your Saturday afternoon plans consume 60 energy units and your Saturday night plans consume 70 energy units. You obviously can't do both—or at least it would be extremely unwise of you.

So what do you do? Skip one and focus on the other, attend one and only part of the other, or skip both and substitute something that consumes fewer energy units.

Planning around the expected expenditure and not your time availability is going to help you budget your energy better so you don't get overwhelmed, because you manage yourself better and don't place yourself in situations to get overwhelmed. Understand your own boundaries and, like the previous point, gain a conscious understanding of what you have been doing to yourself.

If you complain about always being socially exhausted, you might be doing it to yourself without realizing it. Just because your time is free does not mean that you are free!

Try to assign a rough estimate of how many energy units each activity will consume, and give it an honest assessment. If you have only 100 per day, then you'll begin to see how to use them more effectively and budget your days. You can look at it like a game of Tetris with your energy that requires some creative arranging. You might also set yourself a limited number of social activities per week or weekend. Understand your limits and respect them.

If you tend to find yourself overbooked, something that may help with this is to *batch* your interactions together. This means that instead of having an activity on Thursday, Friday, and Saturday, to try to collect the people you were going to see on these three separate days and put them into consecutive activities on Saturday—one right after the other.

You may not get time in between these activities, but you will get plenty of time before and afterward to charge up and recharge. In a sense, you are capitalizing on your momentum and taking care of everything at once, giving yourself larger breaks and less consistent activity. Constant activity can be far more tiring than having one day that you are a bit wary of.

With batching, you are able to create huge cushions to prepare and unwind with. This brings us to the final point in this chapter.

Quiet Bookends

A *bookend* is a standalone piece of wood or metal you place on a bookshelf to keep books upright. They come in sets of two: you would have one bookend on each side of the book, and the book is in the middle like the meat of a sandwich.

If you know that you're going to be subjected to mass socialization, then you should plan your day wisely. Schedule solitude before and after a social event, particularly afterward to deal with the ensuing *social hangover*.

If you know you are going to be social at a certain time, make sure that you get some recharge time before and after it. This way, you'll go into a social situation charged and allow for charging immediately after. You will be able to burn brighter socially at that designated time. For some, this may not be limited to the hours before and after. It might be for even one or two days before and after an event. If you can even grab 10 minutes before and after an activity in complete solitude, this can help immensely.

For example, if you have a big event on Saturday, you might arrange to have solitude on Thursday, Friday, Sunday, and Monday. Schedule these into your calendar or planner with a huge red pen and never deviate from them. Don't even schedule heavy work or anything else that will tax your mental state on days of intense socialization.

Remember, solitude is not just about quantity; quality also matters. The deeper and less interrupted your solitude, the higher the quality and resulting impact on your social battery.

Introvert life design is essentially working around how someone with lower social tolerance can walk the thin line between too much and too little. It can be difficult to strike a balance, but as you've read, it mostly takes a bit of foresight.

Chapter 5. Everyday Situations

Even though our first instinct might be to never leave our homes, we must admit that when we are eventually dragged outside, most of the time we actually enjoy ourselves. It's just that ending bit that annoys us, but we genuinely enjoy the prospect of people and fun activities.

We had better, because we don't live in a world where personal bubbles of plastic are socially acceptable to wear everywhere.

Personally, I am lucky to be able to design my life in many ways like this because I am typically writing or researching, which means I am someone who sits by themselves in silence the vast majority of the time. But not everyone has such power and latitude over our lives

You may not be able to design your everyday life to be ideal for your introverted tendencies, but there are still ways and perspectives with which to approach daily life in a less exhausting and more pleasurable way. Again, this is a chapter on strategy and preparing yourself for the challenges you know will arise from your social battery.

I'm Fine, This Is Just My face

I distinctly remember one networking event from my former life as a lawyer.

It had been going on for three hours, and I had already collected roughly 10 business cards from other lawyers that I was probably just going to toss into the garbage when I got home. I had already asked and answered the question, "So what area of law do you practice?" about 18 million times. I was socially toasted and my face showed it.

One of the servers at the venue walked by and did a double take and then asked me, "Whoa, are you okay? Do you need some water?" Even though I wasn't physically tired, my mental exhaustion showed plainly on my face and caused people to treat me differently.

If you're an introvert, it's likely you've heard this question, or some variation, at some point in your life: "What's wrong? Are you tired?" No, I'm fine. This is just my face when I'm not actively engaged.

When we're not talking to someone, we are prone to shutting off immediately rather than looking around with eager eyes in search of our next interaction. This is going to include our face, body language, and the way we present ourselves. It's the next best thing to going home, after all.

The thing is, when we carry ourselves this way,

we look like unconfident *schlubs*. When you completely let your mental state take over your physical state, you're probably not looking your best. If this is something you want to intentionally convey to people to scare them away from engaging you, that's fine. But most of us are completely unaware of how we look when we are in our introverted heads. Likewise, most of us would like to emanate more openness and positivity no matter the state of our social batteries.

Thus, it becomes important for introverts, whether energized or socially exhausted, to be able to pass the *Mirror Test,* also known as "I am dying inside but at least my face is not."

What does this mean?

It means that you have to monitor, curate, and improve all of your nonverbal communication so you look energized and alert in the mirror even when you are not. Let's look at it this way: tired people sitting at a table lean their heads onto their palms and slouch over. If you do that, you're sending a nonverbal message of boredom and lack of interest in people.

In other words, you need to at least *look* open and personable when you're socially exhausted, or you'll just appear unapproachable and arrogant. Think about it—the type of person you would categorize as "full of themselves" displays the same exact kind of behavior as a tired introvert.

As much as we all know that it's what's inside a person that matters, what shows on the outside and our perception of it still counts. That's just the world we live in. Studies have pegged the totality of communication that is nonverbal to be somewhere between 55–93 percent in various contexts. Whatever the case, it's clear that nonverbal communication is far more important than the actual words that come out of our mouths.

It includes more than just your face—tone of voice, inflection, body language, gestures, body posture, feet positioning, hands positioning, and eyebrow movement. Put all these different signals together, and it can send a message that may be very different from what you want to convey.

So how does the Mirror Test work?

Sit down in front of a mirror and tell the story of your first kiss to yourself out loud. It's a story that should evoke some strong emotions, positive or negative. Really commit to telling this story and going through exactly how it happened and how it made you feel during and afterward. If this isn't a story that has any emotional impact to you, feel free to substitute it with another story you might use to emotionally open up to someone.

Now, focus on how you look in the mirror— your facial expressions and body language.

Did you have energy, or did you have dead eyes, a monotone voice, and slumping posture? Whatever your story evoked, were you able to actually convey those? For instance, if someone couldn't hear you, would they be able to name the emotions you were trying to convey with the first kiss story?

How much effort would it take for you to make 100 percent clear the emotions you want people to feel? That's how you pass the Mirror Test. Despite how you feel inside, you need to simply do better on the outside or you will simply not be received well the majority of the time. The rest of the world doesn't care about your introverted tendencies, only what they can see, and this is an important realization for some.

Many introverts focus too much on the text of what they are saying instead of the context of their words. They think that just because they've gone through the least amount of effort to say the correct words, their job is done and they deserve to be well received. No, text and context go hand in hand, lest you send mixed and confusing signals to people. When you do that, you're in danger of provoking a reaction that is completely different from the reaction you are expecting.

The Mirror Test serves to make sure that even

when your social battery is drained, you are still approachable and a good conversationalist because of the signals you are sending out. Closely related to the Mirror Test is *the Microphone Test*. I'm sure you can guess where this might be going.

The Microphone Test is where you tell the same story, and instead of focusing on how you look, you focus on how you sound. As mentioned, your tone of voice and inflection are large components of the judgments people will make about you. Whether you are tired or energized, are you sounding how you think you are? Are you coming across in a positive manner, and are the emotions you are evoking clear?

Passing these two tests will help you deal with the rigors of daily life much better.

Prioritize

The act of prioritizing also accomplishes something very important—it allows you to feel okay with what you are and are not doing.

People, introverts especially, who have a poor sense of prioritizing often get sucked into things they hate doing or that aren't important whatsoever. This is often coupled with a low sense of self-esteem and self-worth. While those are topics for other books, the advice in this section can be helpful on those fronts as well.

To prioritize and deal with daily life better, make two types of lists: an *"I should stop"* list and an *"It's okay to"* list.

For instance, *I should stop* going to parties where I only know one person, or *it's okay to* ignore requests from casual acquaintances. Your *"I should stop"* list should be what you actively want to stop doing but feel you are bound to do by some duty or obligation beyond yourself. In an ideal world, you would avoid these things because they don't make you happy, or they make you unhappy. For example, you should stop feeling shame or seeking approval for not doing something. *You should stop doing these.*

On the flip side, your "It's okay to" list should contain what you want to do more of, despite what other people might tell you or how they might judge you. You would do these in your ideal world, but you also might feel some sense of duty or obligation not to. They make you happy and give you pleasure. For example, it's okay to skip events, not be the perfect host, and not support every single party your friend throws. *It's okay to do these things and you should do them more*.

Can you see how powerful these little phrases immediately are? They work on two levels. On the first and somewhat more obvious level, they allow you to dissect and examine what you are doing with your life. They subconsciously make you ask questions like:

- What do I really want to do?
- What actually matters?
- Why am I doing something?
- What can I avoid?
- Who is going to be happy from this—is it

me?

- Is this a real priority?
- What's my real motivation or this?

It can be empowering to realize that you actually hate doing something and are only doing it to please your parents. Similarly, you might realize that you love something and only refrain from it because you think your friends might laugh at you. It begs the overall question—who's life are you living?

On the second level, and this is more introvert-specific, understanding your priorities can conserve your social battery in a huge way. Over-commitment and generally engaging socially in things you don't need or want is exhausting. This allows you to pinpoint those things and avoid them. You can't do everything society tells you that you should, and you shouldn't. By telling yourself that it's okay to be your introverted self and staying at home on a Saturday, you'll feel more comfortable and less inadequate. By telling yourself that you should stop going to parties just because you got invited, you'll spend your time in ways that you prefer.

In the act of prioritizing, these two lists also help you prioritize yourself and your own needs over those of others. Only Superman can adequately fulfill his own needs, his significant other's (Lois Lane's) needs, his parents' needs, and every single one of their friends' needs. For the rest of us, we need to choose, and we should make it a habit to choose ourselves.

When you can view your mental state of being as your first priority, your lists might start morphing. Instead of suggestions, these are commandments for you and others to abide by. Instead of "I should stop," it becomes "I absolutely will not." Instead of "It's okay to," it becomes "I won't let anyone stop me from doing this."

Boundaries and Guidelines

We can manage our day-to-day better by instituting *boundaries and guidelines*. You can think of boundaries as the lines you draw in the sand for other people and guidelines as the lines for yourself. They both give you control in the chaotic environments you might find yourself in because you have a role in setting the rules that you are living by.

Boundaries are the ways in which you make yourself unavailable for others. For instance, letting your coworkers gently know that you simply can't handle any impromptu chats before 10:00 am and after 3:00 pm, or whenever it might be. Or your significant other must leave you alone for an hour after you get home (minus saying hello) so you can unwind every day. Or telling friends you won't reply to any messages after 8:00 pm on weekdays. You get the picture.

Boundaries are small steps you can take to reclaim your time and keep your energy higher as a result. A small note on boundaries: when you let others know about them, it's far more productive to tell them your boundary is a "don't" rather than a "can't" because they will be less compelled to question you.

Guidelines are for yourself. They're your own rules for social living. For instance, if you go out two nights in a row, you won't go out for the next three. Or you'll never go out more than four times a week. Or you'll never stay out later than midnight. Or you won't plan any outings for more than five people. These are how to keep to your wits and not get carried away into situations you'll probably hate.

In hindsight, it might be a bit odd that there need to be so many ways to trick yourself into acting in your best interests. But that's how humans function.

Preparation

The final aspect in improving everyday socialization is to prepare as much as possible beforehand. Sounds simple, but there is a surprising number of actions you can prepare the fact.

The reason this is important for introverts is because, to beat a dead horse, socializing is tiring. But it's even more tiring when you have to come up with everything new and fresh right on the spot. For instance, if people ask you about your childhood, it can be tough to draw back into your memory banks and decide what to filter, discuss, omit, and emphasize. But if you already had an answer prepared for this type of question, you could just recite on the fly, as it was rehearsed.

Which is more tiring: reciting a speech or thinking up something new?

Adapting in the heat of the moment is far more fatiguing, so live easier by preparing what you can beforehand. You can prepare:

- Answers and stories to the usual small talk questions you know you will encounter.
- Answers and stories about your background, family, and education.
- Answers and stories about your past weekend and upcoming plans.
- Answers and stories about your job, hobbies, and interests.

- Answers and stories about recent happenings.

We've talked about designing your life to be more introvert-friendly, as well as instituting a few guidelines and rules for the same purpose. These address daily life. Looking ahead, we'll be discussing more specific tactics to milk the most out of social situations.

Chapter 6. Interpersonal Dynamics: Friends, Coworkers, and Lovers

As you might suspect, introverts are somewhat selective about who they spend their time with. This is complicated by the fact that introverts also tend to create unique dynamics because of the way they think and prefer to interact with others.

For instance: the simple inclination to withdraw from close friends, even though they have done nothing wrong. It's just not a frame of mind many people can understand. After all, if you like cake, then don't you want to keep eating cake?

This leads us to the first interpersonal dynamic to be aware of.

Show Consistency

It's obvious but needs to be said. Not all of your friends will think like or understand you, especially when you want your alone time. You're going to be sick of people from time to time. That's okay and that's just your nature.

When you want to withdraw and disappear off the grid, you're going to have to make a concerted effort to not offend people and have them understand that it has nothing to do with them and that it's rather about you. You have to make it known that you feel consistently about them and that you aren't just being moody or angry at them.

Therefore, to create a sense of consistency in your friendships, first make sure they understand your need to withdraw. Then realize that you'll probably be in the position of turning down more invitations than you accept, so make sure you do so graciously and don't repel them just so you can have your solitude. There is a nice way to get solitude and recharge and a not-so-nice way.

The not-so-nice way sounds something like, "Hey, I'm going to go. Sick of hanging out with you. See ya." This sounds comically rude, but when you're socially exhausted, I promise that your exit strategy isn't actually much nicer. Not only does this destroy any semblance of consistency in your friendship, it actively poisons it and creates tension. They thought you liked them, and then you gave them a message like that. What are they supposed to think? It's confusing and frustrating.

The nicer way sounds something like, "Hey, I'm sorry. I know we planned for a little longer but I'm seriously just exhausted. Is it all right with you if we continue this sometime really soon? It's been so great spending time together! Sorry!"

These types of responses can be used in

turning down invitations, leaving social events, and any time you have to indulge in your introverted tendencies. There's a big difference between the two versions. Your relationships will fare much better if you remind them that you like them before disappearing instead of silently vanishing.

Stay consistent in your message on how you feel about them. Don't assume others think like you or even understand you. Introverts have a tendency to internalize their thought processes rather than express them. Whatever they are thinking, you may never know it, but that's probably not intentional. If they're tired, these things will just go unspoken.

In a similar vein, if you like someone as a friend, actually show interest in them in a tangible way. Don't let this go unspoken. What you feel inside might not translate to your physical appearance or actions. You already have proof of this happening because you've probably been told to "cheer up" or "smile more" when you were just standing there feeling normal.

Introverts can often come across as unapproachable or standoffish because they are not effusively warm and welcoming to people. You don't have to be the latter, but don't leave your friends guessing how you feel about them.

Work Dynamics

For introverts, the office can be a minefield of people and meetings to avoid.

It's the epitome of forced interaction and socializing with others, especially if you have the dreaded *open office plan*, which is an office that is essentially one large room full of desks. One room for 50 people and no barriers? That sounds like an introvert's nightmare.

The office can be tricky because you can get constantly distracted and sidetracked by people. Simple things like eating lunch become a chore because you might want to eat alone and relax, but it's impossible to escape people's grasp.

Whether you are consciously or subconsciously acting to extend your social battery at the office, there are certain dynamics at work that can help your cause.

The first dynamic is to speak less yourself and rather through a representative. Imagine you are standing with Tim and Connie.

You: "Tim, how are you?"
Tim looks knowingly at Connie.
Connie: "He just went to Guam! Isn't that cool?"
Tim nods head vigorously

Connie acted as the representative in this simple example, which allows you to see how it can extend to other office situations. Tim was present but did not need to expend any social energy because Connie spoke for him. Connie saved Tim from a bit of social fatigue and would continue to do so if Tim prompted her with a look to answer for him and be his representative

The trick is to make people your representative and speak for you. You can do this officially and explicitly by briefing others ahead of time on the major points that you want to touch upon. For social situations, this is easy and means you just have to tell one person about your weekend, and you can compel them to tell everyone else. Tell one and let them be your megaphone.

For work contexts, it's more difficult, but you can still make people your representative by either giving them credit or acting as if you trust them. For instance, "Connie knows the answer to that better than I do."

As with all introvert tactics, this minimizes the amount of interaction you actually need to do and, especially if your social battery is exhausted, allows you to avoid miscommunication or projecting fatigue.

Another work dynamic to embrace is to replace speaking with writing as much as humanly possible. Sometimes we just want to roll into the office and stay glued to our computers and not talk to anyone at all. Well, get better with communicating through the written word and that can be somewhat possible.

Talking and engaging can be exhausting, but communicating through writing doesn't impose the same drain as having to react to someone face-to-face. Writing also allows you to be more thoughtful and thorough and to choose your words carefully and accurately. You create a paper trail where everything can be tracked and accounted for, and this is great for working in terms and staying organized. It can also help protect you.

In other words, try to institute a policy of communicating by email, text, and letters whenever possible. Then try to make knowledge of your policy widely known.

It can be as simple as saying:
- "Can you shoot me an email on this so I don't forget it?"

- "I have to run right now, but if you email me I promise to look at it ASAP."
- "Let me reply to you via email to give you a better answer."

You can also set boundaries and limitations for when people can or cannot speak to you. If appropriate, you can articulate a headphone policy with a small sign on your desk that says, "If I am wearing headphones, email me first!" Headphones, by the way, will be one of your best shields because they often indicate that you are focusing and less open to distraction. Make sure your headphones are prominent on your desk or head when you wear them.

Whenever possible, try to restrict yourself to text, email, and letters.

Similarly, you can create designated check-in times. You might think that you are actually making things more difficult by introducing specific opportunities for people to fatigue you, but you are actually batching all of your interaction together and gaining freedom for the rest of the day or week.

You may not be the boss, but you can still proactively preempt people interrupting you by, well, interrupting them at a set time. Essentially, this means walking around the office at specific times and giving and receiving updates from everyone you need to hear from twice a day—at the beginning of the day and in the early afternoon. You can also explicitly tell people how you are arranging your schedule so they know what you're doing.

All this amounts to people leaving you alone for most parts of the day because their concerns and questions will have been taken care of in the morning or will be answered in the early afternoon. Exhausting your social battery only twice during the day and letting it recharge in the interim is much better than having people slowly chip away at it throughout the entire day and never having a moment to yourself.

The final office dynamic to capitalize on is to

get in as early as possible. Why? Because this is not a popular thing to do, which means you will be able to avoid people in the mornings. That's extremely valuable alone time that you can avoid social fatigue and distractions from your work at hand.

If you can muster the willpower to get in early, save intensive work for those periods of time. This is for the work that you hate being interrupted on and need some measure of flow to optimally complete. You can reserve the smaller, busy-work tasks that need only a little bit of attention for when people are milling around you.

Introverted Dating Tactics—by Sarah Jones, Founder of Introverted Alpha

[Note from Patrick: I'm pleased to be able to bring you advice from my impressive friend, Sarah Jones, who is the founder of Introverted Alpha. Introverted Alpha has been featured in Forbes, Cosmo, Business Insider, The Huffington Post, San Francisco Chronicle, and more.

Dating, whether you are extroverted or deeply introverted, starts with you and your values. Too many of us seek what we are told we should want without first asking if it's what we actually want as unique individuals. You can probably think of many examples from your own life that fit this pattern.

When we talk about your values, they flow in both ways—that is, what you can offer others and what others can offer you.

One of the first courses of action I recommend is that people start with a large list of values and narrow it to five in order from most to least important. A quick Google search will turn up lists of values online.

Be sure to select what is important to you, not what your friends or acquaintances would tell you is important. This will be challenging, but the idea is to get a strong sense of the priorities you hold for your future relationship and partner.

The next step is to think about what you project outward—what you can offer others. Introverts bring qualities that extroverts don't—most notably mystery, intrigue, thoughtfulness, and a knack for listening well—and it would be a shame if you didn't take advantage of them.

Along with these general introverted traits, what about you specifically is unique and sexually attractive? Don't sell yourself short here—all you have to do is look at the evidence in compliments you've received.

Recall the specific compliments you've received in the following three areas: (1) your physical looks and overall presentation, (2) your interpersonal skills and generally how you make others feel, and (3) your talents or things about you that *you* like. Come up with at least a few for each category, and choose the five that make you most happy and proud.

At this point, you've put thought into who you're looking for and who you are. The next step is to think about what you are absolutely *not* looking for and what traits would be more draining than invigorating for you. Honesty with yourself is key in naming nonnegotiables and deal breakers about someone's values and personality—and sticking to them.

This is especially important for introverts, who can often feel like they're settling for less than they want, simply because it takes so much perceived energy to let something go and pursue another option. When you know what is important to you and stick with it, you'll say yeswith more discernment and save yourself from situations where you're either (a) settling or (b) being passive.

A great way to be more active in a gentle way is to start meeting potential dates in places that cater to your introverted tendencies. Socializing as the first and foremost goal can sometimes feel overwhelming to introverts, so this means focusing on venues that are based on hobbies (dancing, partner dancing, playing volleyball, cycling), education and learning (any type of class like a cooking or language class), or interests and shared values (volunteering, personal development, a certain industry or interest).

More laid-back environments bring out your best for potential dates to see, and they aren't as socially taxing for you because there is always another purpose to fulfill. As a rule of thumb, loud, boisterous spaces are not a flattering backdrop to a more understated, reserved disposition.

Instead, it's best to go where you are genuinely excited to try something new and meet new people. It's that same openness to new things and people that will make you a great first date.

While online dating can be a great complement to meeting people in person, there is something about being social and open to others that is refreshing and confidence-boosting for reserved introverts.

It's important to remember that bars and clubs are not the only option to meet people! I've actually put together a list of over 115 options for in-person, of which bars and clubs are merely two.

You don't have to stay out all night or go to loud, crazy places. A simple cooking class or dance lesson will do.

[Author's note: I'm also a big fan of online dating. I see it as a huge boon for introverts in particular because of the simple fact that it allows people to flirt, get dates, and get to know each other without having to go through tiring social situations up-front. Half of the flirting and draining small talk is instantaneous because you have information available in a profile, and it's easier to get these out of the way before you actually meet face-to-face.

Everything can be done from the quiet and solitude of your own home and laptop.

When you, as an introvert, go out to a bar or party, you probably don't stay out that long. If you do, you certainly aren't in the most open and sociable of moods. If you are searching for other introverts, they also aren't out very long. As you can see, it's just not a situation where the odds are in your favor and you have a high likelihood of creating a romantic connection with someone that shares your interests and values.

Online dating allows all of this, and for those that insist that they want to create romance organically and naturally, I would argue that this is the new organic. Back to Sarah.]

At Introverted Alpha, one of our cornerstone themes is **intentional quality over excessive quantity**. This means that as an introvert, it's going to be more advantageous to focus your energy on a limited amount of connections, so you can give a fuller effort toward the good ones.

The shotgun approach (otherwise known as the numbers game) is a counterproductive move for the introvert because you have limited social energy, so you should use it wisely by only moving forward with someone based on the quality of the interaction.

Moving forward is generally anything that expends additional social energy, which can be something as small as asking an additional question or going deeper in conversation.

Moving forward helps you get out of your own head and into the moment with whoever is in front of you. Introverts are thoughtful, and that is a strength. At the same time, it can seem to be a weakness because left unchecked, it can turn into excessive self-consciousness.

Being too self-conscious can hamper your flirting abilities in two main ways.

First, introverts may have trouble breaking the touch barrier because it can seem too forward. Touch is a natural part of human connections, and a simple light, friendly touch goes a long way toward building an easy-feeling, pleasant connection.

A great moment to do this is to touch gently on the arm or hand when you're sharing a laugh together. It shows whoever you're speaking with that you are comfortable in your own skin and comfortable with connection.

Second, introverts may have trouble with general flirting and reading the *vibe* of other people. There is a tendency is over-analyze small and subtle cues that may not have meant anything. A key is to lay what could be insignificant details to rest (twirling hair, crossing legs) and simply focus on how warm or cold someone is overall: how relaxed and open in body language, breathing, facial expression, and tone of voice. That will be your guide to either get closer or give some space.

While you may feel introversion puts you at a disadvantage, the opposite is actually true. When you learn how to use your focused and introspective nature to form relaxed and thoughtful connections with yourself and others, you'll find your own unique groove and attract people naturally.

You can learn more from Sarah about attracting people naturally at IntrovertedAlpha.com. When you opt into the free training on her website's home page, you'll get her latest and best resources for introverts and dating, including an email series, free PDFs, a video training, and more.

Mixed-Personality Relationships

So what happens after you take Sarah's excellent advice and end up with a mate, introvert or extrovert, who is your opposite temperament?

The extrovert wants to go out and recharge their social battery while doing so has the opposite effect on the introvert, who would rather stay in and re-energize in the peace and quiet of their home. The extrovert also constantly wants to interact and spend time with the introvert, who needs solitude from time to time. Think of the difference between a golden retriever and a fickle cat.

Considering that these opposite perspectives

determine how a significant portion of the time couples are together will be spent, it's worth taking a deeper look.

It's important to know each other's limits. For extroverts, how much time can they spend at home alone or with their introverted partner—watching TV together, sharing a meal, or maybe even not interacting at all? And for the introvert in the relationship, how much socializing is enjoyable, or at least manageable, before it becomes exhausting and overwhelming? If you are with someone long enough, there are definite patterns you can find—if you look for them.

It's a fallacy that extrovert/introvert relationships can succeed if only the introvert becomes more extroverted or the extrovert becomes more introverted. In fact, such a one-sided compromise will almost surely have negative results in the end.

The key here is balance in all respects. Achieving the proper balance means that the introvert has enough down time to feel energized, the extrovert has enough social interaction to feel energized, *and* nobody's feelings get hurt along the way. *That* is the crux of the matter in navigating these relationships.

The best way to find a healthy balance is to engage in activities that feed both people's goals. Introverts are less likely to enjoy spending hours at a crowded club and extroverts may be prone to boredom in situations with lower social requirements or stimulation. What's the healthy medium?

Compromises can range from browsing stores, exploring interesting areas, traveling together, playing video games with or against each other, going to the movie theater instead of watching movies at home, or even pursuing different interests while still enjoying each other's presence in the same physical space. There are so many ways that couples with one introvert and one extrovert can spend plenty of time together while both having their needs fulfilled.

And it is often in these happy-medium activities that the contrasting personality types can really complement each other. Let's take traveling as an example.

The introvert in the relationship may enjoy planning the details of the trip: booking affordable airfare, reading through reviews to find the perfect accommodations, etc. Upon arrival at the destination, the extrovert can take social pressure off of the introvert— making comfortable small talk with the taxi driver or approaching strangers in the hope of making new friends to share the adventures with, to name just a couple examples.

In this way, the travel experience can be better for both partners, as they each get to spend more time doing the things they enjoy while their partner happily does the activities that the other partner considers less desirable.

In order to get the greatest benefit from your relationship, being open-minded and willing to leave your comfort zone can go a long way. Being with your partner and learning about them provides a fantastic opportunity for your own personal development, exposing you to new ideas and ways of thinking that can improve upon your own.

But sometimes, one or both partners have just had enough. What then?

Both members of the relationship need to understand their partner's needs and not take it personally when those needs don't align with what they want. It's not a slight when the introvert doesn't want to attend that office holiday party with their extroverted partner's coworkers, who they barely know, just as it's not a slight when the extrovert decides to spend a night out socializing with friends instead of watching a movie at home. If you imagine that someone loves oranges, and you only have apples, then it's clear that they will have to get their apple indulgence somewhere else.

"I love you, but I don't want to see you right now, and that's okay" is something that is the unspoken mode of operating. Both partners need to feel that they can responsibly manage their own social needs without hurting the other's feelings.

This may all sound easy in principle, but often, putting it into practice when introducing other complex variables can make things tricky. That's why you'll need to set up boundaries about when to accommodate each other and when to take care of yourselves.

Chapter 7. Parties, Hangouts, and Gatherings

Just because I'm not talking and appear disinterested doesn't mean I'm not listening.

I'm not grumpy for no apparent reason. I'm just hungry for solitude. Don't ask me if I'm grumpy because that will actually make me grumpy.

And once again, yes, this is just my face, I'm not exhausted or angry.

Can you imagine having to tell your friends that? It's hard to think of yourself as a social person when all of these things are true. So let's get down to brass tacks. What are the social situations that give introverts just the right amount of socialization for their tolerance? These apply whether you are planning to engage with an introvert or you yourself are an introvert.

Party Planning

Well, first of all, don't call it that. You know, the "P" word. *Party*.

When you invoke this word, even if the event really isn't a party, introverts are going to cower and either avoid it or put their own negative expectations on it. A party is something with huge groups of people, loud music, and inane and shallow conversation. They'll turn up close-minded and already judgmental, and that's just not conducive to making friends. Substitute anything that makes your event sound small and insignificant, such as a get-together, small gathering, hang out, or even meeting.

Actions start with belief, and belief of a relaxing and comfortable atmosphere is what introverts are after.

Your second task in planning a party is to circulate an agenda by email, social media, or any other medium to all of the invitees. As you well know, an agenda is important because it allows you to set your expectations about how your battery will be taxed. It doesn't have to be extremely detailed, but it should tell guests what is involved, how many people will be there, information about the venue, and anything else that will help other introverts be prepared. For instance, there will be extremely loud music at the bar, but there is a balcony and outdoors area in the back that is quieter. These are all helpful to know.

One piece of information that is imperative to include in the agenda is the ending time of the event. This is the light at the end of the tunnel for introverts. If they can just keep hanging on until that time, they've made it! They can pace themselves according to it. Just be sure to make it a little earlier than you actually intend to give people the excuse to leave early if they wish.

The truth is, endless parties are scary propositions. It's like signing a contract without reading any of the important paragraphs. If you're hosting an event at your home, feel free to kick people out ruthlessly. Introverts will secretly be happy if they're told, "You don't have to go home, but you can't stay here!"

Speaking of the invitees, you should make sure to limit their number and also suggest that they are less welcome to invite their own guests. Try to make it so there are relatively few new faces, and that most invitees will know each other or at least recognize each other. Keeping a high ratio of familiar faces is far less taxing socially.

The next aspect about party planning is to make sure there are other ways for guests to be entertained besides through conversation. Parties for introverts shouldn't just be a mass of people gathering in one location. This makes social interaction the only choice of activity, and you risk burning out introverts prematurely because they can't get a break. Simply make sure there are other things the introvert can do while at a party besides talk. This can mean anything from having a theme for the party, having a main activity like bowling or painting, interesting wallpaper or artwork, having a guest speaker or person of focus, or including a movie.

Many introverts ignore socializing altogether because they believe it must include prolonged, intense social interaction with no escape. That does indeed sound exhausting, but that doesn't have to be how you engage with your friends. In fact, it's probably *not* how you engage with your closest friends and family.

You don't need nonstop banter for hours. One way you can ignore convention is to engage in *silent group activities*: spend time together in a way that doesn't require talking. You're basically making the interaction secondary to the activity.

For example, doing puzzles, going for a run, playing soccer, throwing a Frisbee around, knitting, drawing together, playing chess, going to a bookstore, bowling, golfing, or any other activity that can involve at least two people. Engage in these silent activities with others and you won't feel drained. It comes down to smart planning with the motivation being to avoid constant chatter. What other examples of spending time together silently can you come up with?

If the people you are with are introverts, you're all going to be happy for the break. Just remember that friendship chemistry looks different to everyone. The ideal version that is portrayed and idealized in the media is similar to the extrovert ideal, and you know yourself better at this point, so why not deviate?

You can also give your partygoers jobs and duties for the party, which will keep them occupied and give them an excuse to escape people for a bit. It also takes the pressure off them to socialize and chatter, and they just intently focus on ladling out punch without seeing it as a chore—rather, they'll see it as a blessing.

A final aspect of introvert party planning is to proactively cater to them by designating areas as recharging spots, quiet areas, hideaways, getaways, or solitude rooms.

You probably already find these spots yourself—bathrooms are popular for this, as are empty staircases and dark alleys just outside of bars. But these places tend to be deserted because they are weird, dirty, and uncomfortable. You also run the risk of having your fun solitude time spoiled by someone inadvertently walking in and disturbing you. Therefore, having designated areas for you to sit quietly, play with your phone, or just stare into space gets rid of this confusion and allows you to remain undisturbed. Just put up a hand-drawn sign virtually anywhere, and make clear on the ever-so-important agenda that these recharging spots exist. Let introverts find calm without hogging the bathroom.

Hangout Planning

Obviously, there are different types of interactions, and though party planning is important to master, the types of interactions you will have more frequently will be much smaller and low key. Let's call these *hangouts or gatherings*.

Indeed, some introverts might stick exclusively to hangouts and that's perfectly fine. So what are some key guidelines in setting up hangouts with introverts?

First, it can start before you even initiate a hangout.

Introverts are prone to disappearing off the grid for untold amounts of time. If you're an extrovert, this is going to be extremely confusing and like they just vanished. Other introverts will understand their sudden absences. However, you never know what mode they are going to be in that day. They might take a few days to get back to you—it's not personal, they are just shutting out all contact until they feel energized enough to face social settings again.

So give introverts space and time to reply to you when you initiate a hangout. Don't feel insulted, and don't make them feel guilty or obligated. They'll get back to you at their own pace. In the meantime, just be patient and start searching for a venue that meets the requirements of the next point.

Second, pick your environment very carefully.

We know that settings like loud clubs are at the wrong end of the spectrum, but there are a few things you should look for in quieter settings. First, make sure it isn't a tiny place that makes people feel trapped. A lack of physical space can magnify feelings of intensity and exhaustion because there will be nowhere else to look but at the person across from them.

Make sure the time at which you are going isn't crowded or loud with music. Try to avoid places that force you to share tables and benches with strangers. Try to have the environment be in an area where there is space to explore and perhaps a view or even a quiet live band in the background to distract the conversationists. Finally, make sure there is actually a bathroom nearby—the most convenient of recharging stations.

Third, choose the participants carefully.

If you want to hang out with an introvert, hang out with *them*—don't bring along strangers that they have no purpose for meeting. If there's a clear purpose, go right ahead, but if not, you're just making the hangout less and less appealing to an introvert. More and more, it will sound like that party of strangers introverts love to hate.

In fact, try not to bring more than one or two other people even if the introvert knows them well. In other words, keep it small and familiar to create an atmosphere where the introvert will feel welcome and inclined to participate. If there are too many people, or too many new faces, the introvert may fall into observation and passive mode to save their energy. The one benefit of having relatively more people is that if you see an introvert is getting tired, you can shift the focus to other people to give them a slight break.

The fourth point is related. If there are too many new people, we naturally revert back to small talk interview mode.

You know what that sounds like, and you probably hate it. Having a smaller, tight-knit group prevents this and allows conversation to delve deeper into deep topics. As mentioned earlier in the book, try not to hop to a multitude of topics in short succession—when this happens, it's impossible to be anything but shallow. Stay on one topic, dig, dig deeper, and then move on. Keep it meaningful and give them a reason to care; otherwise, you'll lose them.

In the actual conversation, try to let the introvert set the tone and pace. If they appear to be thinking, don't interrupt or rush them or demand a reply. Give them space and only then will they continue to engage without burning out quickly.

Finally, if you sense they are growing tired, there are three easy courses of action you can take.

First, you can turn the conversation onto yourself and be the talker rather than speaker. Most conversation advice will implore you to do the opposite and put the spotlight on the other person, but if that other person is an introvert, the spotlight often gets too hot for them. Give them a break and let them passively participate in the conversation by listening more.

You can also give them a break by retreating to the bathroom yourself, even if you don't need to use it, and let them recharge alone at the table without you.

Finally, you can simply cut the engagement short and declare that you have to stay on your schedule. This may seem rude and abrupt, but if an introvert is growing tired, they will be internally thankful for your initiative and sparing them the tension of making an excuse to leave.

Parties and hangouts can be tricky, but advance planning can make you wildly social *as* an introvert and extremely comforting *to* introverts. One final element to be aware of is FOMO and how you shouldn't let it dictate your actions.

FOMO

The fear of missing out—otherwise known as FOMO—is when you ask yourself if you should do something that you absolutely do not want to do just so you don't miss out on what could be.

FOMO comes about because we idealize what we think we're going to miss out on. We think purely in terms of the potential and possibility and almost never in terms of reality. Of course, there's a *possibility* of meeting supermodels at the party—it's not a zero percent chance. This can be powerful motivation that can give rise to FOMO.

We do it for the fantasy instead of the actual activity.

When the idealized version falls short of the reality, suddenly we're at a social event that we're annoyed to be at. FOMO can lead introverts to their worst social nightmares because we're not out as often, so we tend to wonder in our ignorance. *Is there a secret that all these extroverts know but I don't?* Probably not.

Just ask yourself about the social gathering you are contemplating attending:
- Is it different in any way than other similar events you've been to?
- Will it be fun even if nothing *amazing* happens?
- Is there a high chance of it being *amazing*,

and what would make it *amazing*?

- Will it make you happier at the end of the night, or would you rather have been home?
- Is it being sold to you by people (extroverts) that don't have the same definition of *amazing* as you do?
- Will it have a clear exit plan for you to leave?
- Will it make you regret not going when you wake up the next day?

Chances are, it will be the same situation that you've been in a hundred times and that you know you don't prefer or like as much. It's just going to be the *normal* type of fun that saps your social battery, not the *amazing* fun that you idealize. Is it better to be happy alone or annoyed and tired in the company of others?

We also get FOMO because we face more peer pressure to be social than other people. If not directly from your friends who simply want your company, society still holds the extrovert ideal and sometimes wonders if there is something odd if you don't want to be the social butterfly.

Regardless, you've found yourself there, so what now? The party survival tactics in the next chapter are designed to make parties easier and more manageable for the person who easily fatigues socially. The first party trick, as you just read, is to *just not go* and realize that you truly aren't in the mood.

Chapter 8. Party Survival Tactics

Party tactics are some of the most important things an introvert can learn.

These methods are for those times that you'd rather be home but find yourself at a social event somehow. Maybe you just wanted to be invited and not feel excluded, yet got peer pressured into attending. Or maybe you promised to just drop by and hang out for 20 minutes and can't formulate an escape plan because the door is barricaded by 10 people that you'd have to say goodbye to. Hopefully it's not that you felt like you *shuoldn't* be at home alone on a Saturday night and thus went out to feel better about yourself.

Whatever the case, you're there now. Your introverted tendencies be damned, how can you make the most out of your social events and, dare I say, even enjoy them?

Seek a Role

One of the best ways for an introvert to survive a party is to find themselves a *role*. A role keeps you occupied and, most importantly, gives you something to do other than socializing. If your role at a social gathering is to simply "relax and mingle," this isn't necessarily positive for an introvert.

The funny thing about roles is that they are usually what one would consider work, but when you find yourself in an uncomfortable social situation, you're incredibly grateful for the distraction. They are blessings that are disguised as jobs.

If you're at a bar, your role might be to watch

people's drinks like a hawk and to be in charge of making sure everyone's drink is filled. If you're at a barbecue, your role might be to grill the meat or set up the picnic tables. If you're at a networking event, you can even volunteer and be registering people or giving out nametags. You can also play DJ and be in charge of the music selection or flit around with a camera and proclaim yourself the official photographer of the party. The possibilities are endless, and many of these roles come naturally when you're the one hosting an event.

Having a role is also beneficial because it allows you to interact with people, but not too much. Many roles you'll have will be people-adjacent, so you can interact at your own pace, but ultimately you can keep your focus on your role. It limits your interaction and gives you an excuse anytime you want to leave a conversation. You will always have something to fall back on.

It's a failsafe out, so to speak. Any time you hit a lull in a conversation, you have to go take care of the grill. If you're talking to someone that is boring, or you are getting bored, you have to go take care of the grill. Need to recharge your social battery? Grill time.

If there are no apparent roles available at a social gathering, you can create one for yourself by bringing something you need to set up, create, monitor, or serve. For instance, arriving somewhere and bringing the ingredients of a great dip or bringing a video game or board game you can teach people. Take matters into your own hands and keep yourself entertained as well.

Having a role keeps you busy during a party. It makes the party secondary. Recall that socializing for socializing's sake isn't usually fun for an introvert, so staying busy with things other than socializing can be incredibly gratifying. No more standing around and feeling overwhelmed by people trying to talk to you—you're busy!

If there are truly no roles available, then your

next course of action is to appear *preoccupied*. This is as close to *fake it till you make it* as it gets in this book.

Be *into* something.

Being preoccupied at a party means to be engrossed in something that is happening. For example, if there is a drinking game being played, or a basketball game playing on television, you can actually become interested in it or at least feign interest. Either way, you look busy and occupied, which gives you something to do and prevents people from engaging you as much. Remember that your goal is to preserve your social battery— by being preoccupied, you can use this time to buy yourself some imperfect recharging time.

HIDE

It's easy to hide from people like a skittish cat when you're at home, but the problem arises when you're in a public space.

Whatever your environment, scope out the lay of the land and find quiet areas with little to no people that you can simply hide in. This might be near the exit, a dark alley, a backyard, a hallway, a staircase, or even one of the bathrooms. Think of it like you are casing the joint for a burglary, but in reality, you are figuring out where you can retreat to recharge your social battery incognito.

You've probably done this before by going to the bathroom and noticing how nice it was to have silence and be undisturbed for a bit. Every social area you find yourself in will have a hiding place. It is up to you to put in some effort and energy to find these areas. It's also not a bad idea to simply leave the area and take a stroll outside for a bit if you are in too small and confined of an area.

Once you have a clear idea as to where your social hiding places are, you should visit them frequently for short bursts of time throughout the event or activity. You can be there alone, or you can be there with just one friend (but maybe not in the bathroom).

After an intense conversation, go hide for a bit. If you give a speech, go hide. If you've had to play host, take an extended bathroom break. If you were in the spotlight and told four stories in a row, you know what to do.

This whole process is all about advanced planning and thinking strategically. Your social engagements don't have to end with feeling awkward or burned out. Do it intermittently throughout the evening. Don't wait until the end of the night when you are already exhausted and recharging for 10 minutes won't make a difference. Pop into the bathroom stall for perhaps 10–15 minutes out of every hour or perhaps after every long conversation. The point here is to schedule your breaks to make sure you can stay in a comfortable zone, as opposed to running down to zero.

When you're recharging, to get the most out of it, don't use your phone, don't check your email, and don't do anything that will stimulate you mentally. Remember that it's not necessarily just your social self that is overstimulated—it's you as a whole. Your brain gets tired and overwhelmed and you just want to shut down. Therefore, shut down completely and give your brain a complete break from everything. No consumption of any kind unless it's completely brainless.

Engage Individuals

Group conversations are an interesting proposition for introverts. On one hand, it's nice to be a part of a conversation without having to expend much effort toward it. You can simply *exist* in a group conversation with little to no effort. All you have to do is make a comment or two and laugh accordingly when someone makes a joke.

On the other hand, group conversations can be draining because you have to react to and engage with multiple people at once. These conversations can feel pointless because it's nearly impossible to go deep with a group of people as shallow, relateable topics will always prevail. They will necessarily lack the depth to be interesting to you. And once the spotlight is turned to you, that can be downright intimidating.

To avoid these situations, make an effort to focus on engaging with individuals. Stay away from group conversations and look instead for the people on the *periphery* of group conversations. You can look for people walking about by themselves or people who look as bored or tired as you.

You might even be able to find other introverts in this way, who might be extremely relieved to meet you.

Once you are able to engage with an individual, the next step is to ensure that it remains a one-on-one dialogue and doesn't grow into a group conversation. You can do that by simply prompting the other person to come with you to the edge of the party or a quieter area so you can hear them. You can even just say, "Hey, let's sit over there."

Engaging individuals can also be done

effectively if you position yourself in the venue in such a way to only engage one to two people at a time. For example, you can suggest a smaller table or couch or a narrow hallway. This will make sure that you don't get overwhelmed and give yourself the opportunity to connect on a deeper level with people.

Do Work Beforehand

I would be remiss to not mention that just showing up and implementing these tactics may not always be enough for you to feel like you're succeeding at a party.

There is a lot of work you can perform beforehand to make youself prepared and protect yourself.

First, if possible, bring a chattier friend of yours who engages others easily and energizes you. This wingman or wingwoman will act as your safety valve and be able to keep a conversation going no matter how tired you get. Ideally, this person doesn't mind if you stop talking for minutes at a time and can lighten your load.

Second, impose a time limit on yourself. Don't leave within the first hour, but don't plan to stay more than two or three hours, and make sure you aren't inadvertently staying until the last hour. That two- to three-hour time period is when you're at your best, and anything beyond that will probably be a slow slide into exhaustion. Make an appearance, make an impression, make your presence known, then feel free to leave.

Make sure to set your time limit beforehand, and even tell other people about it so they have the correct expectations about you. "I can only drop by for a couple of hours." The real way that sentence ends is "because I will want to go home and watch three hours of television."

Third, try to make a connection with another guest before the party or event. Try to find out who among your friends is going and make it clear that you'll be there as well. If there is an invite list, you can do this with strangers. Skim the invite list and make a note of whom you have things or connections in common with.

Then either come prepared with that information or reach out before the event with a message like, "Hey, I saw that you know Tim and Candy. That's wild! How did that happen?" If you are able to connect in person before the event, that's even better; you can even plan to go to the event together if you both get along.

Fourth, have an exit plan prepared. In other words, how are you leaving?

Make sure that your exit plan is not contingent on anyone else, because you don't want to have to stick to someone else's schedules or whims. Make sure you can leave on your own and aren't depending on someone for a ride, for instance. Maintain full control over when and how you will leave.

Fifth, it is often advantageous to arrive early.

There are fewer people present, and it will be easier for you to engage individuals and small groups without feeling overwhelmed or tired.

Finally, get warmed up and ready for the event. There is nothing worse than rolling into an event or party and wasting your first three conversations because you weren't awake mentally or vocally. It's like when you are called on in class. You are either ready and alert or you have to think for a second and clear your throat before speaking.

My favorite way to do this is to *read out loud* before heading to a social event. Find a short passage of roughly 200 words, preferably with dialogue, emotion, and different characters. In my coaching practice, I have had clients read a passage from *The Wizard of Oz*.

You want to focus emphasizing and exaggerating the following to the hundredth degree: the emotions, the characters, the volume, the expression, and range. Really perform each scream, laugh, whisper, and question. Pretend you are a kindergarten teacher reading to your class and this will give you a good idea of where to start.

Read this passage three times in a row, each time seeking to eclipse the prior version in terms of outlandishness and cartoonishness. After the third time, you'll be amazed at the difference in your voice and expression.

The Great Escape

A lot of this book is focused on how introverts can make the best of a social interaction, whether they are energized or drained.

But sometimes, you just don't care. You want to leave and hopefully not insult the people you are with in the process. You never know when a goodbye will turn into a 10-minute conversation—this is why many of us actually avoid goodbyes. But if that's how you leave or disengage, you can come off as hostile or socially incompetent. You have to master the art of *bowing out of conversations* gracefully and heading for the exit.

172

The Call

You can tell others you got a call, text, or email that you need to deal with in some way. Not even your close friends or coworkers know the details of your daily obligations and work duties, so it's easy to simply look at your phone and express surprise or concern. Almost no one will have a problem with it because they know that urgent issues pop up all the time. It's perfectly legitimate.

"Excuse me, do you mind if I step out and take this?
"Sorry, I just got something that looks urgent. Do you mind if I head home to take care of this?"

You can also just glance at your phone to see the time and say something like, "Wow, I didn't realize the time. Do you mind if we continue this later? I have to deal with something on a deadline today."

You don't even have to elaborate much on what you are supposedly dealing with. This is a perfectly legitimate-sounding excuse.

The key here is to ask for permission to be excused. It's a gesture of good will. It makes it clear that you are taking the other person into consideration and being courteous so as to not reject them for something else. Besides, it's not like anyone will refuse permission by saying, "No, stay here and talk. I'm more important than your job."

Bathroom Time

You can tell others you need to be excused to use the bathroom. This is a great excuse also because you can just stay in the bathroom for a bit to recharge, as we've discussed.

The best time to do this is about five minutes away from the point where you see your social energy level getting completely wiped out. It should give you enough time to physically get to the bathroom, do your thing, regain your composure, build up your social energy level, and engage people again. It's your choice whether you want to return to that situation or not.

Just make this excuse seem urgent, and they'll completely understand it. Again, this is because literally everyone has felt the sting of the growing water balloon inside them when they have to resist going to the bathroom.

"Wait, I'm sorry. I've been holding my bladder ever since I got here. Can you excuse me?"

Use Someone

You can say that you need to talk to someone else. This may seem like it would be rude, but people have no problem with this if you do it correctly. Again, the key is to make it seem important and urgent.

If you see someone walking by, you could say, "Oh wait, is that Steve? I'm sorry, I need to catch him and I've been calling him constantly. Can you excuse me?" If you're isolated and you don't see anyone walking by, you could say, "I know this is random, but do you think Steve is around? I called him three times and he didn't get back to me. I think I need to check on him. Can you excuse me?"

Pawn

This is when you pawn the person you are talking to off to a friend or someone that is walking by. There are a few steps to this.

First, look around and see who you can pawn this person off to.

Second, try to catch the attention of the other person so they will come your direction. You can also slowly walk your way over to the new person.

Third, when you make contact, introduce the two people to each other. The key to this tactic is to make each person sound incredibly fascinating so they will immediately engage with each other. Introduce each person with one or two of their most interesting traits or experiences, and this should be easy. You're putting yourself in the periphery of the interaction and making the new people the focuses.

"Oh hey, this is Barry. Barry is our resident karaoke master and runs marathons. Michelle had a pig as a pet when she was a child and drinks about four Diet Cokes a day."

Fourth, now that the focus is off you, there is less pressure for you to escape gracefully. All you need to do make a small excuse, like any of the excuses in this chapter, and walk away.

Imagine if the two people are chatting excitedly and you haven't even said anything in a minute or two. You could just say, "Oh, there's Steve. See you, guys!"

The four tactics in leaving I mentioned have a few themes in common, which is why I also want to provide a small framework for the most acceptable way to escape an interaction. If you find yourself in a situation where you can invoke all of these factors, you can escape anything.

First, have an excuse ready to leave any

conversation or social situation. The bathroom, needing to call someone, or searching for someone else always works. It doesn't have to be too specific, just have something ready on the tip of your tongue.

Second, act as if the need for an exit is urgent, so the other people in your context won't take it personally or question it. This is important because we sometimes feel that leaving a conversation is tantamount to rejecting someone. In a way, it is, but we can mask that feeling by conveying urgency and importance. No one is going to feel insulted if you need to go home because your apartment is flooding.

Third, ask for permission and then apologize for having to leave. Drive home how genuine and courteous you are. Show remorse about the fact that you are escaping and they'll feel good about it.

Finally, say something about the future. For example, "Let's do this again soon" or "I want to continue this conversation!" This adds a final level of empathy and care so people can feel good about the fact that you are departing.

As you can see, most of these factors are aimed toward obscuring the fact that you simply don't want to be there anymore and sparing the feelings of the other people. You are conveying your full message but without the negative impact.

These four steps can help you build an exit strategy for wherever you go and whatever situation you find yourself in.

Is it deceptive? Some could see it that way, but if the alternative is to get cornered by someone who lacks the self-awareness to see you yawning while you are already exhausted, making you grumpy and annoyed, then I would choose to convey the message without the impact every time.

These introvert party tactics will help reinvent your feelings toward parties and realize that you can enjoy them just as much as the extrovert at the center of the room—it will just be in a different way.

Conclusion

After I discovered most of what I now know about introverts, it did not take long for me to quickly hop on board.

Actually, I might have hopped on board a little too much and a little too quickly, because I learned that being an introvert was a pretty good excuse to not do anything at all.

As with everything, moderation and a balance is necessary. You might feel that your social battery is perpetually low, and maybe it is. But do not let your labeling turn you into a social hermit because you want to preserve that battery. I made that mistake, and finding the balance may be your biggest challenge yet.

But that is what the survival and party tricks are for. So get out there!

Sincerely,

Patrick King

Social Interaction Specialist and Conversation Coach at
www.PatrickKingConsulting.com

P.S. If you enjoyed this book, please don't be shy and drop me a line, leave a review, or both! I love reading feedback, and reviews are the lifeblood of Kindle books, so they are always welcome and greatly appreciated.

Speaking and Coaching

Imagine going far beyond the contents of this book and dramatically improving the way you interact with the world and the relationships you'll build.

Are you interested in contacting Patrick for:

- A social skills workshop for your workplace
- Speaking engagements on the power of conversation and charisma
- Personalized social skills and conversation coaching

Patrick speaks around the world to help

people improve their lives through the power of building relationships with improved social skills. He is a recognized industry expert, bestselling author, and speaker.

To invite Patrick to speak at your next event or to inquire about coaching, get in touch directly through his website's contact form at http://www.PatrickKingConsulting.com/contact, or contact him directly at Patrick@patrickkingconsulting.com.

Cheat Sheet

Chapter 1. Understanding Introversion

There are a host of misconceptions about introverts that paint them in a negative light. Rather, they are just different—psychologically and biologically. They have very different expectations for social interaction and are ruled by their social batteries.

Chapter 2. Your Surprising Strengths

Just because you grow socially tired doesn't

mean it's all bad. Extroverts also have some significant disadvantages, but introverts are good listeners, are relatively immune to boredom, are great at deep focus and concentration, and have good observational skills.

Chapter 3. Extend Your Social Battery

Your social battery will run no matter what, but you can either increase your capacity or reduce the need for it on a daily basis. You can use silent reactions, become a question master, dive deep past small talk, distract yourself with a secondary purpose, and step out of your comfort zone to grow your battery.

Chapter 4. Introvert Life Design

A few ways to design your life to be more introvert-friendly are to plan around social energy expenditure, understand the different types of social stimulation, stick to predictability, and plan around interests.

Chapter 5. Everyday Situations

These are tips related to how we can better handle ourselves in everyday life. These include passing the Mirror Test, figuring out what you want should prioritize, and setting the boundaries and guidelines you can use to guide your social life.

Chapter 6. Interpersonal Dynamics: Friends, Coworkers, and Lovers

Unique interpersonal dynamics arise with introverts—your friends never quite know if you hate them because you disappear, so become consistent in your message with them. You can also design your office life to be more introvert-friendly, and Sarah Jones chips in with some advice about knowing your values to find a temperament-appropriate mate.

Chapter 7. Parties, Hangouts, and Gatherings

In this chapter, we discussed how to plan an event that is conducive to introvert socializing, such as giving agendas, setting ending times, creating distractions and silent group activities, and providing recharging areas. For more everyday hangouts, it is equally important to choose the participants and environment carefully to not overwhelm and provide space and comfort.

Chapter 8. Party Survival Tactics

You're at the party—now what? Find or create a role for yourself, hide in recharging stations such as bathrooms, engage individuals and not groups, do as much preparation beforehand as possible, and learn the Great Escape—how to gracefully leave a conversation ASAP.

CPSIA information can be obtained
at www.ICGtesting.com
Printed in the USA
BVHW010747131022
649148BV00024B/397